Neem Karoli BABA

An Indian Incarnation of Lord Hanuman
A devotional book for those whose life has become meaningless

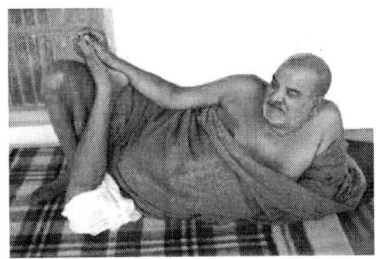

BY
VISHNU RATNA
(Swami Prem Avinashi)

An Osho Disciple
Devotee of Neem Karoli Baba

INDIA · SINGAPORE · MALAYSIA

Notion Press

Old No. 38, New No. 6
McNichols Road, Chetpet
Chennai - 600 031

First Published by Notion Press 2018
Copyright © Vishnu Ratna 2018
All Rights Reserved.

ISBN 978-1-68466-233-3

This book has been published with all efforts taken to make the material error-free after the consent of the author. However, the author and the publisher do not assume and hereby disclaim any liability to any party for any loss, damage, or disruption caused by errors or omissions, whether such errors or omissions result from negligence, accident, or any other cause.

No part of this book may be used, reproduced in any manner whatsoever without written permission from the author, except in the case of brief quotations embodied in critical articles and reviews.

Rama Darbar

Neem Karoli Baba

Dedication

This book is dedicated to those for whom life has become meaningless.

It is for those who have lost all hopes in life, for whom all doors are closed.

It is not for those who are still living with hopes, for whom life is meaningful, who have not experienced utter sorrow and frustrations in life.

If you are living in hopelessness then this book is for you.

At times life takes an adverse turn and an utter hopelessness and meaninglessness arises leading to utter frustration and despondency.

These are the moments when one is closer to truth.

In such a hopeless situation when there is no one to support, there is someone in the spirit form full of divine energy, empathetic that sometimes comes to our rescue **miraculously.**

We cannot see them but we can feel. Feelings are inexpressible.

Who are these divine souls?

We do not know. We cannot know. Yet we can feel.

Once we are rescued trust arises.

This is a true experience.

It is not philosophical.

It is experiential.

Sometimes these spirits visit this planet in human form.

They are not recognised while in human form except by some who stumble upon them accidentally and feel their intense divine energy.

Or we may also say that only those who are capable of receiving such divine energy are pulled by them through some magnetic force unknowingly.

Such divine energy does not vanish even when they leave their physical form.

They are immortal.

We can invoke them by chanting and prayers even when they do not exist in physical form.

And prayers are heard. It works.

This is true spirituality, true religion.

The world needs today such invocation more than ever in the past.

Man has evolved on this planet but has distanced from divinity.

Sorrow and misery bring us closer to God.

This book is an attempt to describe such divine energy. It is based upon author's own experience and is not philosophical.

Miracles *happen in life through prayer, chanting and devotion.*

Trust and you too would be rescued.

"When you are sad or in pain or sick or you witness any cremation then you actually learn the many truths of life"

– Neem Karoli Baba

Contents

Introduction	*ix*
1. Neem Karoli Baba – An Introduction	1
2. Spiritual Practices in India and the Role of Neem Karoli Baba	45
3. Lord Hanuman and Neem Karoli Baba	84
4. Tulsidas, Rama and Hanuman	120
5. Quality of Life on Planet Earth and Need for a Universal God	160
6. Western and Eastern Approaches to Resolve Human Anxiety, Worry and Misery	199
Epilogue	*237*

Introduction

"मनोजवं मारुततुल्यवेगं
जितेन्द्रियं बुद्धिमतां वरिष्ठं
वातात्मजं वानरयूथमुख्यं
श्रीरामदूतं शरणं प्रपद्ये

*Mano-Javam Maaruta-Tulya-Vegam
Jitendriyam Buddhi-Mataam Varistham
Vaata-Atmajam Vaanara-Yootha-Mukhyam
Shriiraama-Dootam Sharanam Prapadye*

Meaning
(I take Refuge in Sri Hanuman)
1: Who is Swift as the Mind and Fast as the Wind,
2: Who is the Master of the Senses, and Honoured for His Excellent Intelligence, Learning and Wisdom,
3: Who is Son of the Wind God and Chief among the Vanaras (Who were part of the Devas incarnated in the species of the monkeys to serve Sri Rama during His Incarnation),
4: To that Messenger of Sri Rama, I take Refuge (by prostrating before him)."

First of all I bow to the divine feet of Lord Hanuman.

I pray to the Lord that He should take away all the troubles of the readers of this book who have shown interest in the Lord.

I am not an established author.

This book is my maiden effort to share my experience with others.

The book has emerged intuitively.

This book is an attempt to help troubled souls who are unable to reconcile to their adverse life circumstances.

I was born in 1947 and came from a family where education was the main profession. My father was a Professor and retired as Director of Higher Education in Uttar Pradesh, India in 1981.

I studied Electronics Engineering and worked in the university and Industry in India.

Later on I went into certification business in India with collaborations from Australian and New Zealand Companies. I also opened offices in India and in Bangkok.

Right from the beginning, I had an intense desire to know about the universe and the forces that govern it. I was pulled by Sri Ramakrishna Paramhans and Swami Vivekananda and often visited Dakshineswar and Belur Math.

India is home to at least nine recognized religions. The major religions practiced in India are Hinduism, Islam, Christianity, Sikhism, Buddhism, Jainism, Zoroastrianism, Judaism and the Baha'i Faith

I was curious to know about various religions and read books and literature concerning different religions.

I wanted to become insider to some organizations having different spiritual practices.

I joined some religious organizations such as Sahaj Yoga, Chinmay Mission, Krishnamurti Foundation, until I stumbled upon Osho and was initiated by him as a disciple. He gave me the Sannyas name "Swami Prem

Avinashi." I used to run a meditation centre by the name "Osho Satpriti Meditation Centre."

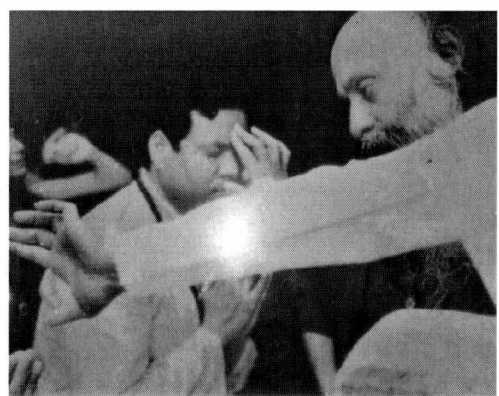

Initiation by Osho

While I enjoyed Satsang and meditation I was not happy with my life.

I had a troubled life both in my profession as well as in my family.

The turbulent life shook me to the core and I did not know how to bring peace.

Religions in India offer different explanations to life's adverse situations. Law of Karma, Past Life, Fate and planetary congregations are theories to rationalize and silence the troubled mind. But this does not solve the problem.

Since 2012, my mental condition deteriorated.

My wife and the only son left me to move to another town (Kolkata) and I was left alone to be on my own in Kanpur. I felt lonely and dejected.

My business was also not running successfully, I was living in a rented house and did not acquire any property since my wife had inherited some properties from her parents and dissuaded me to acquire my own. Following verses of Tulsidas, the famous Indian poet who wrote the epic "Ram Charit Manas" aptly applied to my conditions:

"जहाँ सुमति तहाँ सम्पति नाना; जहाँ कुमति तहाँ बिपति निदाना"

"Janhan Sumati Tahan Sampati Nana |

Jahan Kumati Tahan Bipati Nidana ||

"Where there is love, affection, friendly attitude, cooperation; there is wealth, Lakshmi, prosperity, victory and wellness; on the contrary where there is disharmony one suffers from various miseries."

Me, My wife and Son

My family suffered only because of lack of understanding and harmony amongst members of the small family, myself, my wife and the only son.

My wife foolishly invested crores of rupees that she had inherited from her parents, which she lost and became a pauper. She became sick and died in October 2015 in Kolkata.

My son called me for help. I rushed to Kolkata after the death of my wife and brought my son to live with me in Kanpur.

Having lost everything, I had no house of my own, my son was unemployed and he and his family, (his wife and a son) were financially dependent on my limited resources. All these circumstances in my life kept me worrying.

In January 2017 I was hospitalized and underwent three surgeries.

I was bedridden, became weak and all my activities came to a standstill.

While lying on my bed I used to spend time watching videos on my laptop and reading some literature in the e-book reader.

Neem Karoli Baba came into my life sometime in December 2017.

I started reading more and more about Baba ji. However, there were no books or preaching or recorded lectures of Baba ji which could guide me. Baba ji had left his physical body in 1973 and I had never seen or heard about him during his life time.

The only books and videos available were from his devotees both Indian and western which constituted compiled experiences of various devotees who had met Baba while he was alive.

As I started reading about him and his miracles, I became more and more interested.

In March 2018 I again fell ill. I was diagnosed suffering from colon cancer and was admitted to a cancer hospital in Kanpur for surgery.

I was discharged on April 3, 2018 and was advised to undergo twelve sessions of chemotherapy.

Chemotherapy was an agonizing experience. I could hardly sustain four sessions and gave up after that. The adverse side effects of Chemotherapy shattered my health.

All this time Neem Karoli Baba gripped me and I was reading more and more about him.

Lying on my bed I used to discuss about Baba with my unemployed son Amitabh.

Due to frustrations in his life, Amitabh too was leading a very hopeless life.

Amitabh was a victim of exploitation by the society. He was too naive to face and save himself from exploiters who robbed him and his mother and they became paupers.

He was totally frustrated and on the brink of collapse.

He consulted some astrologers. They advised him to recite Hanuman Chalisa and Sundarkand. They told him that only Lord Hanuman could save him from disaster.

He followed the advice for about 6 months. He used to sit before a picture of Lord Hanuman and prayed regularly. Sometimes he would go to Hanuman temple for prayers and at other times he prayed at home.

Reading about Neem Karoli Baba, I was feeling convinced that he was not only a master but an incarnation of Lord Hanuman. His miracles from the books of his devotees convinced me of some supernatural powers to help solve mundane problems of those suffering from worries. Western devotees called Baba a "Superman" since there does not exist in their religion any concept of "Avatar" or "Incarnation" which is totally alien to them. In India the concept of "Avatar" or "Incarnation" exists and is well accepted.

I had gone to many masters and finally became a disciple of Osho who is the master of masters. He is the only master on this planet who has made all the past masters alive and comprehensible in today's' language.

I used to tell my son that Baba appeared to be an incarnation of Lord Hanuman. He used to listen to me intently.

Baba ji once asked an Indian girl four times: Do you like sorrow or joy? Each time the girl answered "I have never known joy, Maharaj Ji, (He was known both as Baba ji and Maharaj Ji) but only sorrow. " Finally Maharaj Ji said, I love sorrow, it brings one closer to God."

Both my son and I were worried because of various problems. Above words of Baba ji pulled us to him. We were both miserable.

My son showed his desire to visit Kainchi Dham which is the main Ashram of Baba ji near Nainital.

An annual function is held every year on 15th June in Kainchi Dham which is the foundation day of the Ashram. Lakhs of devotees come for Darshan and "Bhandara" (religious feast) on this day and the whole area is overcrowded.

Accommodation in the Ashram is not allowed easily and one has to stay outside. Hotels are expensive and one has to stay either in Nainital or Bhowali or Bhimtal which are at a distance of 15–20 Km.

Neither Amitabh nor I had ever met or saw Baba in his physical form. But I was drawn to Baba and wanted to go myself to Baba's Ashram. Since I was physically unfit, I was unable to travel. I therefore wanted my son to go to the Ashram.

He wanted to stay in the Ashram for two or three days but the Ashram rules were very strict for stay within the Ashram campus. Due to some miracle Sri Pradeep Dixitji who is a devotee of Baba ji in Kanpur helped my son and spoke to the management of the Ashram for permitting Amitabh to stay for 2–3 days. The management agreed reluctantly after some persuasion by Sri Dixitji who was himself a witness to miracles of Baba. Baba used to stay with his family at Kanpur.

My son went to Neem Karoli Baba's ashram on July 3, 2018 and stayed there for three days.

He attended the morning and evening prayers and recited "Sunder Kand" (the fifth episode in Ram Charit Manas written by Goswami Tulsidas") within the premises where Baba lived during his life time. Amitabh felt intense divine energy in the Ashram and great silence.

I am now convinced that the following verse of Tulsidas is true:

"Ab Mohi Bhaya Bharos Hanumanta,

Binu Hari Kripa Milahin Nahin Santa"

Which means: I am now convinced, O Hanuman, that without the Lord's grace one does not come in contact with his messenger (a saint)

Tulsidas also wrote in "Ram Charit Manas":

एहिं कलिकाल न साधन दूजा। जोग जग्य जप तप ब्रत पूजा।।
रामहि सुमिरिअ गाइअ रामहि। संतत सुनिअ राम गुन ग्रामहि।।

"Ehi Kali Kal Na Sadhan Duja,

Jog Jagya Jap Tap Vrat Puja

Ramahi Sumiriya Gaiya Ramahi,

Santat Suniya Ram Guna Gramahi"

Which means that "during the "Kali Yug" (Modern age) there is no other alternative; difficult spiritual practices (Sadhana) and rituals will not be of any help," one should only remember and chant the name of Rama. Saints lovingly listen to His multitudes of attributes.

Amitabh was praying to Lord Hanuman. In India Hanuman is known as a living deity and is called "Sankat Mochan" meaning one who can take troubled souls out of worries. This is not a hypothesis although non believers would scoff it away.

"Deen Dayal Birad Sambhaari, Harhu Nath Mam sankat bhari"

These sacred lines are from Sunderkand of Shri Ramcharitmanas. After burning Lankapuri, Hanuman comes to Mother Sita to ask for further instructions. Sita ji told Hanuman that he should convey this message when he meets Lord (Shriram). Sita ji said, "Say to the Lord that He has been merciful to the troubled therefore ask him to help me out of my present grave trouble."

One can imagine the plight of Sita ji. She had been kept in exile in Lanka by Ravana and had suffered intense agonies.

Hanuman is the central character in Ram Charit Manas. Without him it was not possible to rescue Sita.

Those who are in trouble, if they recite and pray to Lord Rama and Hanuman with full trust and faith, their troubles would start vanishing soon

I am of firm belief that the world today needs people to invoke Lord Hanuman through chanting, prayer and devotion. This would save troubled souls as the Lord is merciful.

Hanuman is a devotee of Lord Rama. Rama is an incarnation of God Vishnu. Hanuman is an incarnation of Lord Shiva.

The Gods when they incarnate in human form, visit this planet from time to time to prevent it from extinction and to help the troubled souls.

Today this planet is on the brink of disaster. Nuclear weapons are the greatest danger. Man is faced with anxiety and worries all over the world.

Neem Karoli Baba is said to be an incarnation of Lord Hanuman. His message was love. He was love personified. People were attracted to him because of his love. He would not allow anyone to go without sumptuous "Prasad" or eatables. His only message was to chant and recite "Sita – Ram Sita – Ram" "Hanuman Chalisa" and "Sunder Kand."

Devotion comes through trust. But trust does not come with wish or mere desires. And without desires or wish no one would pray. This is a vicious circle.

How can one develop trust without desires?

Neem Karoli Baba knew the human psychology. He knew that those who came to him came with some problems. And unless their mundane problems and worries were removed they would not have faith or trust in Lord Hanuman or Rama.

He had the power to know the past and future. He would often tell the person about his problems and why he was there. He would tell the name of the person without any previous introduction. This would surprise the person. And he would say "Go and take Prasad and your problems would be solved." Thus the person would instantly become his devotee. A trust would arise in him. This happened when he was alive in physical form.

But even after he left his body in 1973 people came to his Ashram and their worries were solved. For example Steve Jobs CEO of Apple came to India and visited the Ashram in 1974, after Baba had left his body. He was in great trouble at that time. After he went back to USA soon his fortune started building up and Apple became one of the biggest names in industry.

Mark Zukerberg Founder of Face Book was also in trouble, his company was on sale. He was advised to visit Kainchi Dham. Mark visited India in 2015 much after Baba had left his body. His worries were overcome when he returned.

Jobs had told Zukerberg that in order to reconnect with what he believed as the mission of the company he should visit this temple that he had gone to in India, early on in his evolution of thinking about what he wanted Apple and his vision of the future to be.

Tulsidas in Ram Charit Manas (in Sunderkand) has said:

> *"Sunahu pavanasuta rahani hamari, jimi da1sannhi mahu jibha bichari.*
>
> *Taata kabahu mohi jani anatha, karihahi krip1a bhanukula natha."*
>
> *Hear, O son of the wind-god, how I am living here: my plight is similar to that of the poor tongue that lives in the midst of the teeth. Will the Lord of the solar race, dear friend, ever show His grace to me?*

The context is a dialogue between Vibhishan (Ravana's brother) and Lord Hanuman.

This is very relevant in today's world. We are also living like Vibhishan surrounded by evil forces. Without the grace of Lord Hanuman trust in the Lord would not arise.

Neem Karoli Baba attracted only those who were capable of receiving his grace. He did not invite people by giving discourses, or discussing philosophy. He pulled like a magnet only those who were capable of receiving his grace.

I was more thrilled reading about the divine energy of Baba from the books of his devotees and his miracles and was feeling the intense energy myself.

Baba was an embodiment of divine energy. Those who stumbled upon him accidentally felt an intense energy around him without any "Sadhana" (spiritual practices) and were immediately transformed.

Once someone asked Baba in Kainchi Ashram "Baba you don't preach any Satsang (sitting with a Sat Guru)

Baba said this is true Satsang. "Aao, Khao aur Jao" meaning thereby "come eat and go." Baba ji never imposed any preaching, order or Satsang on his devotees. He never made disciples but those who came in his contact were instantly transformed and became devotees without any Sadhana.

Baba told that Sadhana or spiritual practices are too difficult for an ordinary person. He told that one who goes for spiritual practices would become mad.

He used to say "Only recite Sita – Ram Sita – Ram." By reciting "Sita – Ram Sita – Ram" you would one day become a true devotee or "Bhakta." Even if you have no faith or belief in these words utter them mechanically and one day you would stumble upon true "Rama."

By devotion or Bhakti he meant "Rama Nam." The name of Rama is greater than "Rama" in whatever form he may be "Ramayana" Sunder Kand" or Hanuman Chalisa" (verses from Ram Charit Manas by Goswami

Tulsidas (1511–1623) an Indian poet who wrote the epic in 1575). This was the only way to realize Baba, Ram or Hanuman.

Through such recitation, one day Baba would catch hold of you. You have to walk one step and Baba would move forward ten steps to come closer to you.

India is full of different spiritual practices such as Yoga, Tantra, Meditation etc but Baba would never discuss about these although he was himself a Mahayogi and true devotee of Rama and Hanuman.

I had never prayed in my life. I was not a devotee but only a disciple of an enlightened master. I had meditated but never surrendered. Meditation is a form of "Gyan Yoga." Gyan Yoga, Karma Yoga and Bhakti Yoga are the broad ways of Yoga which is an ancient system for raising consciousness for spiritual growth.

I had no faith in prayer and never visited any temple in my life. I was never into Bhakti Yoga.

During my cancer surgery my sister Kiran Vidyarthi who lives in Indore consulted Sri Raj Kumar Joshiji who is a devotee of Lord Mahadeva and offers prayers selflessly for those who are troubled and come in contact with him.

Sri Joshi had undertaken an adventure to Kailash Mansarovar in the Himalayas, at the young age of 26, considered by Hindus as the abode of Lord Shiva or Mahadeva. This place is at an altitude of 19,000 feet and Sri Joshi spent his hard earned money for this pilgrimage. Sri Joshi has acquired spiritual powers through prayer and has helped many selflessly.

Sri Joshi ji was very kind to me; he promised to pray Lord Mahadeva for my recovery.

Shortly afterwards the adverse side effects of Chemotherapy started reducing and I started recovering.

I saw the miracles of prayer. Once again I wish to repeat that I firmly believe what Tulsidas wrote in Ramcharitmanas to be true:-

"AB MOHI BHAYA BHAROS HANUMANTA,

BINU HARI KIRPA MILAHIN NAHI SANTA"

Without the mercy of Lord Hanuman I could not have met respected Joshi ji whose selfless prayers worked upon me miraculously… and also, today while writing this book I feel that without the mercy of Lord Hanuman it was not possible for me to reach Baba ji…

I am convinced about the efficacy of prayer.

This book is by someone who had never seen or met Baba.

I wish the readers of this book to carry the message of Baba,"Come, Eat and Go "and recite the name of "Sita – Ram Sita – Ram."

That is all and one day you shall stumble upon true "Rama."

Upon Amitabh's return I felt intuitively to write a book about my experiences.

On July 11, 2018 I searched some publishers on the Internet and stumbled upon Notion Press in Chennai India. I was helped by Mr. Pravin Raj about the whole process.

I signed the agreement on July 12, 2018 and paid him advance.

The writing of the manuscript started on July 13, 2018 after I received templates from Mr. Pravin Raj. I thank him for his kind support.

A book is often composed intellectually.

This book is not written intellectually. It is intuitive and based on my experience.

Experience comes out of feeling. Heart is the door to divine.

Today with the growth of science and technology the world has lost touch with the heart. We have lost feelings towards human beings leave alone other creatures inhabiting this planet. Love has become a meaningless word. We live more in intellect, reasoning and logic. Heart knows no logic; it is illogical.

The result of intellectual growth is obvious. Mass murder, hatred, economics, entertainment, competition, consumerism have dominated human life and words like love, God, divinity have lost meaning and become rituals like Sunday prayers.

I also feel blessed that Baba ji pulled me to him by his grace which resulted in Amitabh visiting his Ashram and my writing this book.

I was already a disciple of a master. But I never travelled on the path of devotion. My master gave me the name "Prem Avinashi" which means indestructible love. My path was the path of devotion, love and surrender. But I chose the path of meditation.

Osho

Osho has spoken on almost all the enlightened masters on this planet. He has opened all the keys. But the decision to choose the path has been left to the disciples. A seeker will have to choose for his growth between Meditation and Prayer. This is where the difficulty arises. I chose the path of meditation but failed because my path was that of devotion. He had rightly given me the name "Prem Avinashi" which is the path of love, devotion and prayer.

There are two paths: The path of will and the path of surrender.

Meditation is the path of will. For meditators no God or deity is required.

For a meditator there is no God outside. The God is within. Hindus call it Atman. Atman is inside and Parmatman outside in the universe. Every creature is endowed with Atman or divine energy which can be discovered through meditation. "Aham Brahmasmi" is the declaration of the meditator after he has discovered the Atman within.

Buddha and Mahavira denied God. Their path was the path of will. But there followers started worshiping Buddha and Mahavira because the path of will is not easy. Buddhists now recite the following prayer:

> *"Buddham sharanam gacchami*
> *I go to the Buddha for refuge*
>
> *Dhammam sharanam gacchami*
> *I go to the Dhamma for refuge*
>
> *Sangham sharanam gacchami*
> *I go to the Sangha for refuge."*

Buddha had preached meditation, not prayer.

A seeker needs support of a master, without any external support one cannot grow consciousness.

I did receive silence during meditation but it soon vanished when I faced life's challenges in adverse situations. It was difficult for me to accept the circumstances silently and to watch without identification all that was happening around. I was crestfallen. I used to apply my mind and rationalize the circumstances but always fell victim of my own thoughts.

Path of devotion requires a divine support from some divine energy outside. It requires surrender to a deity. India has opened all the doors for realization – meditation as well as prayer. One has to choose between the two for growth. At the end of the journey both meet at the same point.

Buddha and Mahavira initiated and made disciples. Osho also made disciples.

Neem Karoli Baba never made disciples, whosoever came in contact with him became a devotee. A devotee is on a higher ladder than a disciple.

I also made no efforts but the miracle happened. I am now a devotee of Neem Karoli Baba without having ever met or seen him.

It seems it was destined for me and I had to pass through a long journey as a seeker. I studied in University of Allahabad from 1965–68. Baba used to visit Allahabad quite frequently and lived with a professor of the University (Dada Mukherjee) very close to my hostel. He used to come to Prayag for Kumbha Mela. I also used to go to Kumbha Mela in 1966 but I never knew anything about Baba. Baba was not known publicly and he was against any publicity.

Between, 1968–1971, my father was posted in Nainital. We used to live in Anand Nivas quite close to India Hotel-which was owned by Ma Siddhi's husband. Ma Siddhi was an ardent devotee of Baba. A tenant from Australia used to live in a portion of our house. I am sure she was a devotee of Baba but we never exchanged notes. In 1984 I was asked to set up a Cordless Telephone Project in Jeolikote which is close to Kainchi Ashram but I never went there even though I may have passed several times from that road.

Thus I was not chosen by Baba during my spiritual journey while he was alive. Since Baba was against any publicity, he was not much known in his lifetime except by a few devotees who were drawn to him from time to time. They experienced his love and were transformed without any spiritual practice. The devotees consisted of high and low. Baba made no distinctions between Presidents, Prime Ministers, politicians, bureaucrats, Indians, and Westerners. People of different faiths came to him and experienced divinity.

Even after he left his physical body people have been experiencing his energy.

I have come in contact with many Indian devotees who had never seen or met Baba while he was alive. They all shared their experiences charged with emotion and feeling and how they were transformed.

I feel myself lucky to have come in contact with Baba's divine energy at the fag end of my life.

This is a miracle.

Lying on my bed, having never been to his Ashram, having never met or seen him I feel enveloped by his divine energy. This is my personal experience.

I wish to thank Amitabh my son and Kiran Vidyarthi my sister who brought me in contact with Raj Kumar Joshiji. Sri Raj Kumar Joshiji through his prayers to Mahadeva Ji helped me to recover from adverse side effects of chemotherapy. He also helped me to become a devotee and shift my focus from a meditation to devotion and surrender.

I am also thankful to several devotees of Babaji who helped me to write this book, those who had met and seen Baba physically while he was alive and also those who never met or saw him physically. They all shared their experiences which enriched me. I also wish to thank Sri Pradip Dixtji for helping my son to go to Kainchi Dham.

There are many books written by both Indian and western devotees who had seen and met Baba while he was alive.

I offer my gratitude to all those devotees whose experiences in their books inspired me to know about Baba. Without reading these books I would have never come to know about Baba. There are no books or preaching's from Baba. I would specially like to thank the authors of the book " Alaukik Yathartha," "Miracles of Love," "I and My Father are One" and "Sometimes Brilliant" which helped me to know about Baba.

I am grateful to my master "Osho" who helped me in my journey to come in touch with Neem Karoli Baba. The divine spirits of "Osho" and Neem Karoli Baba are inspiring me to express my feelings through this book. Both these are no longer in their physical body but I can feel their intense divine energy.

I have also used some internet resources including Wikipedia in writing this book. I also wish to extend my thanks to all the contributors on the internet unknown to me for their valuable support.

There may be some factual errors in this book. I wish to make it clear to my readers that I am more concerned about truth than fact and therefore if the facts have to be distorted to point out a truth, this should be accepted. Fiction, fact and truth are three facets of communication. It is not a book of fiction, or of facts. It is to convey some truth based on one's experience.

This book is primarily intended for the western readers who are not much aware about spirituality and often travel to India in search of a Guru. They need guidance to discern the real Master and to avoid the company of false masters who abound in this country to misguide the gullible.

I have to use many Hindi texts in this book. To the extent possible, I have tried to translate the verses in English but at some places that translation was not possible. However, the meaning of these Hindi verses has been explained in English for the western readers to understand the verses.

And finally I thank Sri Dinesh Singh Ji for his valuable support in editing this book and giving his valuable suggestions.

This book is from someone who never met or saw Baba ji in his lifetime never went to his Ashrams or temples and is bedridden with a deadly disease.

I hope this book would help those who are troubled with mundane problems, and have lost all hopes.

Baba used to say "Why worry when I am there?"

Baba exists even now in invisible form and helps troubled souls without the need of any spiritual practice.

Vishnu Ratna

(Swami Prem Avinashi)
An Osho Disciple
Devotee of Neem Karoli Baba
E-mail: ratnavishnu@gmail.com
Mobile: 91-9415101244

Amitabh Ratna S/o Vishnu Ratna
E-mail: amitabhratna17@gmail.com
Mobile: 91-9554976571
Kanpur (India)

July 13, 2018

1
Neem Karoli Baba – An Introduction

There is no biography of Neem Karoli Baba.

Very few facts are known about him, but there are many stories.

This is true of many Indian enlightened masters. Nobody knows about the age of Devaraha baba.

The date of birth of Neem Karoli Baba is not known.

It is presumed that Baba was born around 1900.

He left his body on 11 Sep 1973.

Baba was born in Akbarpur district Firozabad (Admn division Agra) Uttar Pradesh India around CE 1900 in a Brahmin family. His name was Lakshmi Narain Sharma. His father was Durga Prasad Sharma.

He was married at the early age of 11. Due to some reasons he left home a little after his marriage and became a wandering monk.

He had no schooling whatsoever. Baba used to say that everybody in this world already comes educated and God is the greatest teacher.

He was a Siddha, an ascetic already enlightened.

It is said that he went to Gujarat and lived with a saint who gave him the name Lakshman Das. He remained in Gujarat for about 7 years. He grew big hairs and except for a begging bowl and a "langot" (A lion-cloth), had no other belongings.

He also lived in a village 40 km off Morvi in Gujarat, the Ashram of Rama Bai and did spiritual practice in a "Talab" or pond.

After leaving Bavania, he travelled through India and reached "Neeb Karori" a village in district Farrukhabad in Uttar Pradesh.

His voice was very sweet and anything that he uttered was found to be true.

An early photograph of Baba

The villagers loved him and started caring for him. They requested Baba to settle down in their village and constructed an underground cave for his spiritual practice or "Sadhana." Baba used to remain in the cave for Sadhana during the day and came out only during the night. His activities were not known and he remained almost hidden from the villagers.

Later on, due to natural reasons this cave was lost. It was discovered after about 60 years due to the efforts of Siddhi Ma, his ardent devotee, and the cave has been preserved for posterity.

About 200 meters beyond this cave another cave was constructed which is preserved even today. Above this cave a Hanuman temple was set up by Baba. A big feast or Bhandara was arranged for about a month. Baba changed his dress, shaved his hair and wore a Dhoti half covering his lower part and the upper part of the body.

After construction of the temple, Baba came in contact with the villagers. He did many "Leelas" or divine plays which are still popular in the village.

All the young men of the village came in close contact with Baba. Baba participated in different games with the youth. Baba became so intimate that it was difficult to understand his bizarre divine plays. He would play "Hide and Seek" game and would find anyone who was hiding in the forest but became invisible to others. He climbed a tree and when someone followed to catch him, he would soon be found on another tree. Soon he would become invisible. He would disappear in a pond and soon vanish.

Baba was known as Lakshman Das in Neem Karori village. Once, Baba arrived at Farrukhabad railway station from the Neem Karori village where he was engaged in spiritual practices. He boarded a train in the first class compartment. Those were the days when India was under the British rule. An Anglo-India conductor, finding his dress that of a Sadhu, asked him to get down at a small station. Baba alighted from the train.

After that it became difficult for the train to move. The train remained at the station for about two hours. The employees of the station kept on moving here and there. When asked for the reason, the driver of the train said that there was no fault in the engine which was well functioning but the wheels would simply not move. The driver was unable to explain the reason.

All the compartments of the train were examined to find the reason but in vain. Some employees who were moving on the platform came to Baba and mockingly requested him to move the train.

Baba said, "You have thrown me out and now asking me to start the train"

The employees said, "You might be travelling without a ticket."

At this, Baba produced several first class tickets. The employees requested Baba to board the train and requested him to start the train. Baba ordered after which the train started.

It was not unusual for Baba. He helped millions to start their lives which had stopped moving.

It was here that Baba became to be known as Neem Karori Baba instead of Lakshman Das.

Nibkarori Railway station

Baba Lakshmandas Puri Railway station

Later, at the request of the villagers, government of India named in Neeb Karori village a railway station as Baba Lakshmandas Puri Railway station.

Around 1935 Baba moved to Kilaghat a place in Fathehgarh (Uttar Pradesh) near the river Ganga. Baba became popular with the public in Kilaghat. After this, he started moving around to other places and did not stay at one place for a long time. The whereabouts of Baba before moving to Nainital in 1940's is not much known. But he was gaining popularity in nearby towns like Bareilly, Haldwani, Almora, Nainital, Lucknow, Kanpur, Vrindavan, Allahabad, Delhi, and Shimla and also down south in Chennai (then known as Madras).

Baba in hanuman temple at Neem Karori

Many people from poor and middle class families started becoming his devotees in large numbers. He became a divine energy for people of all faiths, Hindus, Muslims, Sikhs, Christians, men and women, young and old, Indian and western. President V.V. Giri, Vice President Gopal Swaroop Pathak, Governor K.M. Munshi, Lt Governor Bhagwan Sahay, Raja Bhadri, Justice Vasudev Mukherjee, Industrialist Jugal Kishore Birla, Poet Sumitra Nandan Pant, leaders of various political parties, Dr. Richard Alpert of USA (now known as Ram Dass) etc paid reverential visits to him. Jawaharlal Nehru, the first Indian Prime Minister met Baba through Sri Bhagwan Sahay. People from armed forces, Police and Civil Services became ardent devotees of Baba. Baba's devotees' were not limited only to males. Once, a male member became a devotee of Baba, his entire family joined along with him. It is difficult to prepare a list of devotees of Baba. It is surprising that people from India and elsewhere in the world were inspired by Baba without any publicity of any sort. Thus Baba made a big family of devotes which included everyone without distinction of caste, creed, religion or nationality.

During the fourth decade of the 20th century, Baba adopted Nainital for constructing a Hanuman temple and an Ashram. He often visited Nainital though he never lived there permanently. Wherever he moved, people followed him from their houses or shops as if they were pulled by some magnetic force. A passerby would leave his work and follow Baba ji due to his attraction. If Baba visited a family, the entire atmosphere became charged, which is difficult to describe through words. Sometimes he would stay in the house of some devotee but mostly he used to stay about 2 Km off Nainital on the Manora hills which was lonely or spent nights on the road. Thus he would give preference to this part of the mountain. People habitual of a family life often accompanied Baba during the night time and remained awake but despite this they did not show any slackness during their daily activities; on the contrary they worked with rejuvenated energy.

Baba established a temple in Hanumangarh and this was the beginning of his further activities.

He constructed temples and Ashrams in Bhumiadhar, Kainchi, Kakari Ghat, Kanpur, Shimla, Lucknow, Vrindavan, and Delhi. Baba used to move about in these places from time to time. He handed over these temples and Ashrams to various trusts and did not have any relationship afterwards for managing them. Whenever Baba visited any place during construction of these temples there would be huge gatherings around him and people witnessed his divine plays.

Baba lived a very simple life always helping others. He would help anyone totally unknown to him whom he met on the way. He would often solve the problems without the person ever asking about it. Indirectly he would help many, his face would often change which was due to his activities both direct and indirect. He had no desire of his own whatsoever. He showered his love on everyone. He could not see anybody in sorrow or distress. He would himself visit the house of anyone who suffered and through his divine power helped to solve their worries. He helped innumerable people in different ways. He helped many to be educated, arranged marriages, gave his blessings to the childless, diseased, and poor and gave life even to the dead. His work was unimaginable and beyond words. People were surprised the way he removed their worries. For him there was nothing impossible.

Baba with his devotees

On September 11, 1973 Baba left his mortal body willingly in Ramakrishna Mission Hospital Vrindavan.

Baba is still helping many even after leaving his physical body. The author has discussed with many such people in India who had never met or seen him but have been helped and they have become his devotees.

It is one of the most mysterious events in the world's history of a divine play in human form.

Baba with western devotees

Baba was endowed with mysterious divine energies. His divine body was always a source of divine plays which are often wrongly described as "Miracles."

Baba's voice was sweet, his vision was divine and his touch could transmit divine energy. Once a person came in his contact his entire family would join and become a devotee. Baba could read thoughts and enjoyed the inner conflicts within one's mind. He appeared to know about a new – comer whom he had never seen or met and would often tell the names of his relatives. He could know the past, present and future of the person before him. He had the miraculous power to predict and his predictions would always be found true without fail.

In India religious scriptures called "Puranas" describe divine energies through mythological stories. These stories often appear to be a work of fiction and are unbelievable. For example, the story of Hanuman described in epics and "Purana" scriptures that Hanuman could fly the ocean and make his body small and big appear to many a work of fiction and imagination. Very few devotees accept and have faith in such stories and others only accept it because these stories belong to the ancient remote past. But Baba manifested these descriptions of Hanuman. Baba could be seen at many places at the same time. Baba could reach to any troubled devotee without any vehicle instantly. These stories appear unbelievable but there are many eye witnesses still alive who have seen these happenings. The author has himself talked to many devotees who were a witnesses to such things and these are also described in some books by devotees of Baba both Indian and western. The author never met or saw Baba in his physical form but has been in touch with many devotees who never saw Baba in his physical form, yet they are receiving the divine grace of Baba even after he left his physical body.

A number of saints and enlightened masters have described Baba as "Power of Powers" or "Light of Lights." People had visions of Baba in different forms depending upon their faith. Someone would see Lord Shiva in him, some as Rama, some as Hanuman, and some as Ma Durga. Baba could reveal himself in a variety of forms which was sometimes confusing. It is difficult to define Baba due to his mystical ways. Even leaving his mortal frame is also said to be his divine play to disappear from the public eye. In short, he proved the belief in divine incarnation of spirit in human form.

Baba was always hiding his divine form. All those who incarnated on this planet have tried in some way or the other to hide their true being but it is difficult to hide their divinity from those who came in contact with such divine beings.

Baba always tried to remain in hiding. Baba moved amongst people completely unknown. Baba remained in Uttar Pradesh for over 50 years but his name remained changing and nobody knew that the real name of Neem Karoli Baba was Lakshmi Narayan Sharma. In India he is called Neeb Karori Baba, in west he is called "Neem Karoli Baba." He was also known as Baba Lakshman Das.

In response to a question by a devotee Baba said that if people would know his true reality, he would be cut to pieces and people would wear his bones around their body as a garland or locket. It is true. The mortal remains of Baba are still used by many to cure difficult diseases.

Baba by helping those in trouble would immediately convert an atheist to become a theist and would sow the seeds of devotion and service in him. A true devotee could never hide from Baba and Baba was always found helping him in his spiritual growth. He would move to many Ashrams and caves and would help seekers by his divine grace.

Thus Baba worked through individuals and not through groups. He never preached or gave sermons. He would often say that these are only linguistic gymnastics. When someone would press him for his message and preaching's he would simply say "I am not educated." Thus he sowed the seeds of highest values amongst his devotees.

Baba did not mind respect or disrespect shown to him; he was above any kind of praise or humiliation. For violation of traffic rules he would bear the brunt of the traffic police – even abuse or manhandling. On the contrary he would help the policeman if there was any public complaint against him, protect and defend him until he became free. He would show generosity even to those who humiliated him.

Baba did not show any kind of hypocrisy so that people would pay respect thinking him to be a saint. He would not paste his forehead with sandalwood nor wore any mala or any dress typical of saints in India. He wore only a dhoti to cover his body like any ordinary villager in India. Later he started putting a blanket around his body. He wore no footwear. It was therefore difficult to recognize him. Sometimes if an outsider would come and enquire about Baba he would simply brush him aside and say "There is no Baba here, go and pray Hanuman ji." He did not want to influence anyone. He met all and sundry like a simple man.

Baba was not in favor of any publicity. Anyone who tried to praise him to make him popular would be asked to go away. If a devotee brought someone for a Darshan of Baba and said anything in praise, Baba would soon utter words that would give a wrong impression to the newcomer and the devotee would feel surprised. Despite this he was becoming popular around the world. People from India and outside who came for Darshan would become his devotees and started praying.

Baba had no greed or attachment for wealth. But he sought the help of the wealthy for construction of temples and Ashrams. If someone poor gave him any donation, he would gladly accept with grace. He was very careful about the use of money and materials but had no greed or attachment. After the construction of a temple or Ashram he would hand it over to a trust for management and did not have any relationship with the establishment after that. He did not accept any money from foreigners, even though at times he would raise a demand that was difficult to be met. The purpose of such demands was only to remove the good feelings from the heart of the outsider. Baba had no interest in these temples or Ashrams. He would spend his nights in lonely places in mountain or forest. He constructed these temples for the sole purpose of common people or householders or Sadhus for prayers in this age of consumerism which is eating into the fabric of society by losing trust in divine energy.

Baba surrounded by devotees

Baba would often show his temper in a unique way. It was difficult to face him when he showed anger. He would often use unparliamentary language and even manhandled the person. This would not only scare the person to whom he showed anger but would also make others fearful. But his anger was of a different kind. After the event was over, he would again be very kind and merciful. Knowing full well his behavior, it was difficult to face his anger. This included prominent persons also. His anger was a way of love.

It is beyond any doubt that Baba was above sex. He set up an example before the Indian saints who were not permitting females to come closer to them. They tried their best to remain away from the opposite sex. On the contrary, Baba had devotees which included both males and females. This also included both Indians as well as foreigners. Baba would catch hold the hand of females or would shake their nose playfully. Such acts did not show anything unusual to visitors. Males were seen massaging the feet of Baba and this was equally true of the female devotees. Everyone felt grateful to Baba to serve him. Baba considered every one as a part of his family. He would often say to the householders "You are unable to take the responsibility of a few children, see I have so many children to look after."

There was another reason for Baba to mix up with the females. He did not grace only the males with his divine energy but the females also who were living a neglected life in the male dominated society. Special privileges were given to females for their spiritual growth. They participated in all the activities of the Ashram and rendered their service in a motherly way. They were known as "Ma" and they progressed much more in spiritual growth compared to males. Service is an easy way for spiritual growth and "Ma's" have a natural instinct towards serving others.

Baba would praise those females who were devoted to their families and kept harmony. On the contrary, he disliked those women who were quarrelsome and created disharmony in the family. He would often say, "Whatsoever be the quality of the husband, it is the duty of the wife to keep the family united, such wives who are surrendered to their husband and family are the greatest Yogis."

Baba before the Ashram

Baba was an embodiment of love. True love does not demand anything in return; it has its own power. Baba did not serve for any selfish motive. That was the reason why people from all over the world were attracted to him. His love was such that everyone would think he was special for him and thought Baba was only for him. Baba never maintained distance from anyone. He remained in close contact with young and old, male and female, Indian and western, Hindus and Muslims without any discrimination whatsoever.

Devotees looked at Baba with great trust and Baba treated them with great love. Everybody felt free to discuss with Baba and no one was scared of him. Baba poured his love, gave them "Prasad" to eat, laughed and made others laugh.

Although a visitor had full freedom to talk anything with Baba, yet he would discuss only that which Baba would like to listen, he would often forget if Baba was not interested in the subject. People met him as if Baba was a family member and they were children to Baba. Baba would address everyone as if they were dear to them.

Baba believed in "Vasudhaiva Kutumbakam" which is a Sanskrit phrase which means "the world is one family." He used to stay with householders and was treated like a member of the family, not a guest. As an elder member of the family he listened to mundane problems with great interest and gave advice besides indirectly helping them to resolve the problem. He could enter the house of anyone without invitation of the head of the family. His purpose was only to help, not to raise demand for anything.

Baba believed that man was a helpless creature. His empathy was with those who were gripped with mundane problems which caused anxiety and worry. His aim was to somehow rid the person from complex problems that worried him. He would even at times help in settling the marriage of a girl and would advice the right groom or bride suitable for them. Some people did not like such a behavior of Baba. They believed that saints should not intervene in worldly matters and devote only to spirituality. Such persons were ignorant about the spirituality of Baba.

Saints are compassionate; they always work for the welfare for others. Baba had no discrimination towards anyone. If due to lack of finances a person was unable to wed his daughter, Baba would come to his rescue and rid the person from his worries. If the circumstances were unfavorable, Baba would make it favorable through his grace.

He was a fatherly figure. He could not see anybody suffer. He worked to remove obstacles physical, divine and material.

Tulsidas wrote in Ramcharit Manas:

"दैहिक दैविक भौतिक तापा। राम राज नहिं काहुहि ब्यापा॥"

"Daihik Daivik Bhautik Tapa, Ram Rajya Nahin Kahuhi Vyapa"

"In 'Ramrajya' there is no physical, divine and material worry."

Baba removed all obstacles using his divine powers. At times he would take the physical disease of someone suffering upon in his own body and would bear it without the knowledge of others. He revived life in someone who died untimely. However, he accepted timely death as the will of the providence.

It was difficult to predict when his grace would descend on someone and the reason for this. It was seen that in a hospital a person would die in the presence of Baba and the dying person was so overwhelmed leaving his body in the presence of Baba that he would die with folded hands and depart from the world.

Baba never expected anything in return for his benevolence. He would often do his work indirectly. If due to some reason he had to shower grace directly then he would go away soon not giving the person any opportunity to thank.

Man remembers God when he is in grief. But Baba would appear from nowhere if he heard the grief-stricken person's voice. He was always prepared to care for even petty interests of persons.

By nature, Baba was caring for poor and downtrodden who became popular through his grace. He chose places which were neglected, forsaken and waste lands for construction of temples which became very popular on account of special features.

It was Baba's grace that an atheist like Richard Alpert, an American psychoanalyst who experimented in the religious use of psychedelic drugs was transformed to become "Ram Dass." Baba believed in humanism as the foundation of spirituality.

Baba had unique quality of forgiveness. He never looked down upon anyone for evil deeds. He would feign ignorance knowing full well the character of the person. He knew that sex, anger, lust, possessiveness, greed and attachments were human weaknesses. He never gave importance to crimes arising out of such weaknesses. He would even forgive a person who stole things of the Ashram out of greed and at times returned the stolen items to him. If someone ill-treated the person for such crimes, Baba would feel hurt. Due to his large heartedness Baba would help an aggrieved person seeking his help for punishment by the government for committing a crime. He would make the person confess his guilt and ensured that he repented for his act. A person who appeared in Baba's court would not receive punishment even by the juries of the court. Such was his way of dealing even criminals. This kind of jurisprudence should be a matter of research by the legal experts because punishment does not reform the person committing a crime.

Baba always remained fearless. Physical, material or divine problems could never create any fear in him. He would spend nights in lonely jungles with great joy. He never feared ferocious animals in the forest. He was able to circumvent any hindrances in his work through government rules and regulations in helping people or for construction of temples and Ashrams.

Baba lived a non-possessive life. He was never worried about his livelihood. He wore only a Dhoti and covered himself with a blanket. He did not have any clothing other than what he wore. If some devotee would gift him a dhoti, he would leave the previous one as a "Prasad" to him. If he did not take a bath for a week, there was no question of changing his dhoti.

Baba believed in reincarnation. He would often say that we meet someone in life only as a coincidence with those with whom we had been related in a previous life. This meeting is for an unknown period after which we depart. Generosity was a quality that we are born with on account of good deeds of the past. "It is difficult to help others through our sufferings, and such an act is on account of good deeds of the past," Baba would say.

Baba never demanded anything; he only shared his joy by giving. His life was so simple that it was difficult to imagine his needs. He said, "We are all poor before God." Through his miracles he would produce currency notes of Reserve Bank, converted water into milk or petrol.

He would use his divine powers only in special situations to help others.

To grow the feeling of service, inculcate the importance of sacrifice, he would ask rich people for construction of temples, Ashrams or arrange "Bhandara" (religious feast) and help the poor and downtrodden.

Baba was very generous to young people and children. He cared for the children and youth and inculcated in them respect for their parents by telling stories. He would never ask anyone to give up addictions, but in his company the addictions would wither away, on its own, without any moral teachings.

Baba was a vegetarian but accepted food from his devotees whether Muslims, Christians, Sikhs or Hindus without any discrimination.

Baba did everything with a purpose. If he went to someone and ate food, that person was helped in the worldly affairs as well as in his spiritual growth.

Baba was very jovial and took interest in sharing laughter. His face had a magnetic charm which attracted the visitors immensely. He was also an adept in the art of weeping. If someone recited Ramayana or Sunderkand, tears would start flowing and he would be drowned emotionally. He would start weeping incessantly. If someone came to Baba weeping, Baba would also weep and tears would come to his eyes. Such sensitivity is seldom seen in the saints and householders. Those emotional, especially the females, would start sobbing and crying with a touch of Baba and would shed tears with a choked voice.

Baba had left his home at a very early age. He had not been educated. His knowledge of Hindi was preliminary. Many enlightened masters like Jesus, Mohammed, Ramakrishna, Kabir and many others were also not educated but they received recognition amongst people. Baba had a unique quality to understand the expressions of language of any country. Very often he would give reply to a foreigner even before the interpreter told to Baba. Once while in Hanumangarh temple in Nainital, he spoke to two Germans for about an hour without an interpreter. The devotees were watching this from a distance. Both the Germans were talking to Baba smiling and laughing and left fully satisfied.

Baba was not interested in accumulating knowledge through words. He never preached, or gave discourses. His discussions were so interesting that it would keep the visitor spellbound. He loved everyone and said, "I don't make disciples, only devotees."

Baba often said, "Once I catch hold of someone, I don't leave him even if he leaves me." This meant that once he showered his grace on someone, he looked after his welfare even if the person forgot him in altered situations. The grace of Baba would remain as such. He was not hungry of anyone's appreciation. This is true even today because people have tremendous trust in Baba even after his leaving the body.

Baba never discriminated on account of different religious traditions, creed, or caste. Hindu, Muslims, Sikhs, Christians, young, old, male, female were all devotees of Baba and Baba showered his grace on everyone equally. Baba was never in favor of religious conversion. He always encouraged trust in their respective traditions and bestowed his grace without any discrimination. He said, "Fundamentally, all religions are one and take everyone towards God." "All human beings are equal, the same blood flows in everyone from the heart to the body," Baba said. He would tell the importance of Islam to Muslims, to the Christians about Jesus and to the Sikhs about their Gurus. While speaking about Jesus to the Christians his eyes would shed tears and he would be emotionally choked.

At the insistence of the Indian ambassador Sri Kidwai, he visited Mecca. With his Christian devotees he visited Church and went to different temples with devotees of other faith. He respected all religions equally. He never opposed any religions but was also not influenced by any religion. He never participated in any religious functions of temples and Ashrams and remained away from the rituals even though the burden of managing the affairs was entirely upon him.

Baba was never seen to practice any Yogasanas, Puja, and Jap, spiritual practices or worship in temples.

All the verses in Ram Charit Manas about Rama were seen manifested in Baba. Baba would often say," Ram and Krishna are no longer with us but the name of Rama would always remain with us. By reciting the name of Rama all the mundane problems are solved." This would infuse confidence amongst his devotees.

About God, Baba would say, "God is fully present in the nature; he is omnipresent and never disappears from our eyes." "If we are unable to see God, it is due to our limited vision, because of our parochial outlook and impure mind," Baba said.

He would often say "because of impure mind and lack of love we cannot feel God."

When someone asked Baba, "If we cannot pray God because of lack of trust, then is it not hypocrisy?"

To this, Baba would retort, "You cannot pray with trust, you do not also wish to pray falsely, then what do you want to do?"

He would say, "In the beginning one can start with disbelief, later with the purity of heart a trust would arise." "To see God one needs to develop an insight, God cannot be seen with the external eyes" Baba would say.

"Prayer and devotion are desirable. Utter the name of Rama mechanically and one day you shall stumble upon true Rama," Baba said.

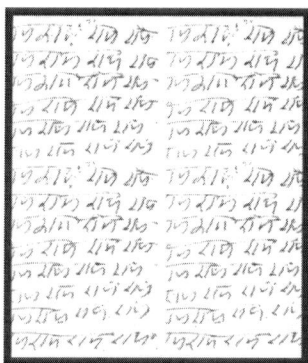

Baba's handwritten "Rama, Rama"

"Trust comes with the grace of God. One has no command and control on His trust. He may shower His grace or take it away, it does not come authoritatively. Ego is the greatest barrier. The entire universe is our home; all the inhabitants are one family. Instead of trying to find God in some form, it is better to see it in everything," Baba said.

Baba would say, "God is the only doer, man is a helpless creature. Why beg before man, what can man give? Saints and God are fully capable but you don't have to demand from them, they are omnipresent and give whatever is needed."

For him surrender to God was the only means to live a healthy, happy and worry free life.

Baba helped millions but was never seen worried. He never sought advice from anyone and everything happened according to his will. He said, "Trust in God does the miracle, everything happens. Man's effort is not sufficient."

Baba's trust in God was so intense that even the strongest atheist who came in contact with him transformed into theism. The materialist Dr. Richard Alpert of America became a spiritualist and was named as "Ram Dass."

If Baba felt that a strong atheist would not change his standpoint, he was able to change his attitude, through his divine play. Once, while in the Vrindavan Ashram, he made tears to flow out of the Hanuman statue; and in Kainchi Ashram made a Hanuman statue drink one container of milk. These miracles were Baba's divine plays or "Lila" which he used to bring trust in God.

Baba considered meditation as important for spiritual growth but if a visitor sat before him to meditate; he would intervene and brought him out of meditation.

Baba understood the capacity of the visitor and knew his own height and depth which he had attained through meditative practices.

In this context, once Baba said, "You are rooted in your body. Spiritual growth is possible through gradual methods, if you enforce it, you may go mad. It is true that concentration does provide insight to realize God but for those who remember God and devote in selfless service, meditation or prayer is not necessary. This is the simplest method for realization."

Sitting close to Baba, his "Darshan" (auspicious sight) and touch was enough to transport a seeker to exalted states. Baba's sight was blissful, his body movements were attractive and his voice was magical. Even if he scolded someone, the person would not leave him. He would often say, "You come to me only because you love me."

It is true that householders attached to the family affairs were not capable of sharing love with Baba; they came to him only for their selfish motives. But Baba did not mind it; he showered his love on them equally. He distributed "Prasad" to everyone who came to him. There was a continuous gathering of people coming and going.

Baba's "Satsang" in simple terms was "Come, eat and go." "Satsang" means sitting close to an enlightened master. One can bathe in the divine energy without any communication. It is a communion. Baba never gave any discourses, his method was simply, "Come, eat and go."

Through his supernatural powers he was able to care for everyone who came to him.

Baba enjoyed giving answers to everyone's questions. He took special interest in solving the mundane problems of everyone.

People raised questions on variety of subjects, political, social, spiritual, individual, yoga, devotion, morality, ethics etc. Baba's reply was very brief, simple and lucid even on complex issues. The questioner would be hypnotized with his answers. He was able to perceive into past, present and future. His replies were spontaneous; he was not required to think. Sometimes he would reply even before the questioner had completed the question.

Baba was an open book. Anyone could read him but it was difficult to comprehend his depth. He was beyond any attributes and dualities. It seems as if he was born in human form to develop trust in a higher being which is beyond comprehension of human mind. He was visible to the eyes yet remained invisible. His form was visible and his divine plays were invisible. He was capable of being omnipresent, omniscient and omnipotent.

In short, Baba's life showed God in human form to his devotees. An inquisitive person would know the unimaginable potentiality of Baba and the truth of divinity.

Although Baba went through various difficult spiritual practices during first half of his life, he did not advocate these to his devotees. For him, remembering God and service to life was the easiest way for realization.

Feeling of service in the Ashrams and the remembrance of God in the temples comes naturally. To inculcate this practice, Baba constructed beautiful, clean and peaceful Ashrams and temples at many places.

Ashrams & Hanuman Temples

It is believed that Baba established first Hanuman temple when he was engaged in spiritual practice in the village Bavania, 40 Km off Morvi town in Gujarat. At that time he was practicing in a pond in the Ashram of Rambai. This statue of Hanuman came up in the open near the pond. Around 1916, Baba moved to north India. Later, a member of Srimat Ramchandra shewetambar Jain constructed a small temple which can be seen today.

In the following pages, I wish to describe about a few temples constructed by Baba or later by his devotees.

Bavania Ashram & Hanuman Temple

Bavania Ashram & Hanuman Temple

More than 100 years ago, after leaving His home when He was quite young, Maharaj ji went to the village of Bavania where there was a Vaishnav saint and stayed there for 6–7 years.

Maharaj ji practiced austerities, Sadhana, and yoga here. This ashram has a pond where Maharaj ji sat and where He kept away from the world. Because of this, Maharaj ji was known as 'Talaiya Baba' then.

There was a tree where the herders who came to graze cattle and goats hung their food. When they went to eat the food, it was gone. They threw stones in the pond while demanding their food. Maharaj ji, sitting in the lake, then tossed various foods, including sweets, to them on the shore.

Neeb Karori Hanuman Temple

Nib Karori Ashram and Maharajji's Cave

Maharaj ji is reported to have sat here on the edge of the village of Neeb Karori, in Uttar Pradesh, as a Sadhu for approximately 20 years until 1938.

The Hanuman temple here is the mandir of Hanuman murti as made by Maharaj ji with his own hands.

The ashram/cave area is less than half kilometer from Lakshmandas Puri railway station where Maharaj ji performed the very famous Lila with the train.

The best known of Maharajji's names as Neem Karoli Baba, Baba Nib Karori (Baba Neeb Karori) is derived from this place.

It was a very remote place then and even now it is off the beaten path.

Hanumangarh Nainital

Hanumangarh temple

Inaugurated in 1951, this is reportedly the first temple established by Maharaj-ji.

This extensive ridge top temple has exquisite views on a clear day.

Hanumangarh temple is about 2 km from Naini Tal. It's a nice walk if the skies are clear. If it's raining you can go by car.

Arati is performed daily, morning and in the evening.

On certain days specific devotional practices such as Hanuman Chalisa are done.

There is a conveniently located sweet shop just outside the gate so you can purchase your Prasad.

There is an ashram here but only Indian staff is permitted is stay in the ashram.

Bhumiadhar Ashram & Hanuman Mandir

Bhumiadhar Ashram & Hanuman Mandir

Maharajji's Bhumiadhar Ashram is a small ashram in the Kumaon Hills near Maharajji's Kainchi Ashram.

Hanumanji was inaugurated in 1967, and Maharaj-ji frequently stayed there.

There are several stories about events that happened with Maharaj-ji at this ashram.

Maharaj-ji often stayed at this ashram while westerners were staying at Kainchi.

The small ashram is located on the side of a steep hill with a beautiful view.

This ashram has one very sweet Hanuman murti. It offers no lodgings, but is very excellent for a day visit from Nainital or Kainchi Ashram.

Kainchi Ashram

Kainchi Ashram and temple

Kainchi is a beautiful secluded mountain ashram located in the Kumaon Hills in Uttarakhand. The first temple was inaugurated in June 1964. Many hundreds of people visit the temples here every day, in season.

Each year, during the famous June 15th Bhandara, reportedly, more than one lakh (100,000) people are fed. Rules are strictly enforced and individuals staying at the ashram are required to participate in morning and evening Arati. While the temples are open to everyone from 7am to 6pm in winter, the ashram is closed for 4–5 months, because it becomes very cold.

It was some time in 1962 when Maharaj ji called for Shri Poornanand of Kainchi village while he himself waited sitting on parapet wall by the road side near Kainchi. When he came, they refreshed the memories of their first meeting which they had 20 years back in 1942. They discussed about the place around. Maharaj ji wanted to see the place where Sadhu Premi Baba and Sombari Maharaj had lived and performed Yagyas. The forest was cleared and Maharaj ji asked for the construction of a Chabootara (rectangular platform) covering the Yagyashala. Maharaj ji contacted the then "conservator of forests" and took possession of the requisite land on lease.

The Hanuman temple is built over the platform mentioned above. His devotees started coming from different places and a chain of Bhandara, kirtans, bhajans started. The Pran-Pratishtha of idols of Hanumanji and others was performed on 15th June in different years. Thus, 15th June is celebrated every year as Pratishtha Divas when a large number of devotees come to Kainchi and get Prasad. The number of devotees and the associated vehicular traffic is so large that the district administration has to make special arrangement to regulate the same. Accordingly some changes have been made in the whole complex so that people do not face any difficulty in movement.

Kainchi temple is of a special importance in each and every devotee's life. It was here that Ram Dass and other westerners spent a lot of good time with Maharaj ji. All devotees should pay a visit to this temple at least once.

Construction of Maharajji's Temple at Kainchi

Maharajji's Temple at Kainchi

Baba ji left His physical body in the night of 10 September 1973. The Kalash containing His ashes was already installed in Shri Kainchi dham. Then, without any plan and design, the construction work of Baba's temple began in 1974. All His devotees cooperated (voluntarily).

The artisans and masons engaged in the construction work had an early bath and wearing clean clothes began work, reciting Hanuman Chalisa and chanting "Maharaj ji Ki Jai" (glory to Maharaj ji). When the construction work was on, the devotees also recited Hanuman Chalisa and did Kirtans by singing (Shri Rama – Jai Rama – Jai Jai Rama); Mothers also writing "Ramnam" on the bricks passed them on to the workers. The whole atmosphere vibrated with the chanting of "Baba Neem Karoli Maharaj Ki Jai." Influenced by the ardent devotion of the Mothers for Baba ji, the workers also developed the same feeling of devotion, faith, reverence and love. It was Babaji's Lila that he infused these workers with the qualities of Vishwakarma (the architect of Gods) and they remained busy with the construction work.

Now came 15th June 1976, the day for installation and consecration of Maharajji's murti. Maharaj ji Himself had fixed June 15th as the consecration of Kainchidham. The Bhagwat saptah and yajna etc. were completed before the installation and consecration ceremony. The devotees installed Kalash and hoisted flag on the temple with the sound of bells, gongs, drums and conches. The sky vibrated with the sound of clapping, Kirtans and slogans of glory to Baba ji. The atmosphere was ecstatic and everyone had the feeling of Baba ji Maharaj's physical presence. Then with recitation of hymns from Vedas and with the specified method of consecration ceremony and worship, Maharajji's murti was installed. In this way, Baba ji Maharaj in the form of a murti is seated in Shri Kainchi Dham.

Kakrighat Temple

Kakrighat Temple

Kakrighat is situated on the road to Almora from Nainital near about 20 km from Kainchi ashram. A river flows along its eastern boundary.

Sombari Baba MahaSamadhi Asthan and remains of his previous Lila place (Old Hut, Raj Asan, Lingam and Holy Trees) is well preserved.

Nowadays the place as an Ashram is under management of Shri Neem Karoli Baba's Kainchi Dham Ashram – Neem Karoli Baba lived and meditated at this place.

Here at Kakrighat, in 1890, during his travel to the Himalayas, Swami Vivekananda sat for meditation under a Pipal tree. Here he experienced the oneness of the universe, of the microcosm and macrocosm, and realized that in the microcosm of the body exist everything that is there in the entire universe.

Hanuman Temple Pithoragarh

After establishing the temple at Kakrighat, another temple at Pithoragarh was established with the cooperation of government officials. On Deshehra day in 1970, a function was organized near water works in Pithoragarh on a mountain top. People believe that after Hanuman statue was installed in this temple, the prosperity in this area grew. Initially it was only a sub-division of Almora district but it has now become a modern district in the northern borders of India.

Panki Hanuman Temple in Kanpur

Panki Hanuman Temple in Kanpur

Inaugurated in January 1964, Panki Hanuman Temple is a very small temple on the outskirts of the city of Kanpur, near Panki Railway Station.

Within this temple resides the very wonderful and delightful Panki Hanuman-ji.

It was said that during the Bhandara feast held at the inauguration of this temple Maharaj-ji was capable of feeding the whole city of Kanpur (population approx 50-lakh, or 5 million).

A MahaSamadhi Bhandara is held here shortly after the MahaSamadhi Bhandara in Vrindavan.

There are no accommodations here whatsoever at this time.

Lucknow Ashram – Hanuman Sethu Mandir

Lucknow Ashram – Hanuman Sethu Mandir

Inaugurated on January 26, 1967, this ashram includes 2 Neem Karoli Baba murti, 2 Hanuman murti, and 2 Shiva Linga.

This temple performs a major service in distributing Maharaj-Ji's Prasad in Lucknow, and seems to be one of the most visited temples in the city.

The ashram is always decorated as for a Bhandara, thanks to a devoted staff. Maharaj-ji said that Lucknow Sankat Mochan Hanuman-ji (known as "the wish fulfilling Hanuman") is "the Governor General of all Hanuman's."

Shimla – Sankatamochana Hanuman Temple

Shimla – Sankatamochana Hanuman Temple

This remote mountain temple was begun many years ago by Maharaj-ji.

This temple is now undergoing a major renovation.

A new Neem Karoli Baba murti was made in Jaipur. This Maharaj-ji murti has a wonderful, high view of all the surrounding area.

At the entrance to this very special temple grounds is a very good Ganesh Temple with wonderful carvings on the outer walls.

Inauguration of the new Maharaj-ji murti was done at Hanuman Jayanti, 1999.

Vrindavan Ashram

Located a short drive south of Delhi in north central India, Maharajji's beautiful Vrindavan ashram is the likely the most propitious of the ashrams and temples of Maharaj ji Neem Karoli Baba. The temple at the cremation place of Maharajji's last known body is called Samadhi Stahl. A yatra to this very holy place is always of great benefit to all devotees.

It was in Vrindavan that Maharaj ji chose to leave His body in 1973. The Neeb Karori Baba Vrindavan Ashram is located in Krishna's holy city of Vrindavan on the plains of Uttar Pradesh. The first temple was inaugurated in 1967. This ashram is on Parikrama Marg a short ways from Mathura Road.

Within this ashram is the MahaSamadhi Mandir of Neem Karoli Baba/Neeb Karori Baba. This is the site of Maharaj-Ji's MahaSamadhi Bhandara in September each year. In this ashram are Hanuman Temple, Durga Devi Temple, Sita Ram Temple, Shiva Yugshala Temple, and Maharajji's MahaSamadhi Temple.

Vrindavan Ashram

Mehrauli Ashram

The Delhi temple is located in Jaunapur near Mehrauli. It is situated amongst huge real estates and is built in a large area. This temple supports a hospital and two schools.

Mehrauli Ashram, Delhi

Delhi Ashram has many murti, including the second biggest Annapurna Mandir in India with a series of delightful bells to be rung as devotees climb the stairs up and also on the way down. Delhi Ashram is noted for its spirit of giving. This ashram has created a hospital and two schools. This ashram feeds schoolchildren every day. In January 2001, a large new goshala (dairy) was inaugurated here.

This ashram is the source of many photos and books about Maharaj-ji. Maharaj-Ji's Delhi Ashram is about one half hour drive southwest of New Delhi to Mehrauli. Outside of Mehrauli you go to Jonapur on Mandi Road past the farms and the village about 2 km on the left.

North Delhi Hanuman Temple

North Delhi Hanuman Temple

This little temple is hidden beneath a flyover of Mahatma Gandhi Marg near the Yamuna River in North New Delhi.

Inaugurated on December 4, 1965, this temple is now almost 'secret.'

It is very difficult to find with a very obscure entrance in an unlikely place just north of the Ladakh Tibetan Market.

This temple along with the small ashram was built by Maharaj ji and funded by Jugal Kishore Birla, who had no children and left his fortune to various religious trusts.

Before the temple was built, Maharaj ji said that there was an old Hanuman murti (statue) buried in the ground at the spot where this Hanumanji temple is located.

The murti was dug up and now sits in front of Hanuman within the temple.

The pujari and 'caretaker' of this temple is named Sri Narayan Swami. The temple is operated by his family, under the Hanuman Ashram Society, one of J. K. Birla's religious trusts.

Each morning Swamiji completes Arati at this temple and travels by auto rickshaw to Maharajji's South Delhi Ashram for Arati and pujari seva, a distance of some 35 kilometers (22 miles). In the evening, Swamiji returns to Baba's North Delhi Ashram by auto rickshaw for evening Arati.

This temple is very deserving of contributions to be directed toward maintenance, plastering, painting, and upkeep.

Rishikesh Ashram

Rishikesh Ashram

Neem Karoli Baba Rishikesh Ashram, just south of Rishikesh, on the west side of the road you will be greeted by one of the two Hanuman murti at Neem Karoli Baba's (Baba Neeb Karori's) Rishikesh Ashram. This Hanuman rises forty feet above the passing motorists so that everyone who enters Rishikesh from Hardwar can have the Darshan of Sri Hanuman-ji.

A beautiful new library of spiritual knowledge has been established at this ashram.

Taos Hanuman Temple, USA

Taos Hanuman Temple is within the Sri Neem Karoli Baba Ashram in Taos, New Mexico USA. The Taos Hanuman Temple is operated by western devotees of Neem Karoli Baba. Of the many gathering places of Neem Karoli Baba Satsang in America, Neem Karoli Baba Ashram in Taos is the home of Sri Taos Hanuman-ji, a most unique and loveable murti.

Maharaj-Ji's Taos Hanuman Temple is located at 7000-ft. elevation in the Sangre de Christo (Blood of Christ) Range of the Rocky Mountains. Taos is a small town noted as a "spiritual center." Thousands of Hindus from all over the world make pilgrimages to have the Darshan of Sri Taos Hanuman-ji.

Taos Hanuman Temple, USA

Darshan of Sri Taos Hanuman

Temples Built by Neeb Karori Baba Devotees

Akbarpur Temple

Akbarpur Temple

This place has a very special importance as Maharaj ji was born in this village. It is referred to as his Janma Sthal. Akbarpur is a very small village in the Firozabad district of the state of Uttar Pradesh, India.

Jabalpur Temple

Jabalpur Temple

The work on this temple in Madhya Pradesh started on 24th Feb, 1997. It is beautifully located on the banks of the river Narmada.

Mirzapur Temple

Mirzapur Temple

This temple is in the Mirzapur district of Uttar Pradesh. This place is very famous because of the Vindhyavasini temple. It is quite close to Benares and Allahabad.

Hanuman Foundation USA

The Hanuman Foundation was established in 1974 by, Ram Dass, the American devotee of Neem Karoli Baba.

The Hanuman Foundation is focused on the spiritual well-being of society through education, media and community service programs.

Subsequently, Seva Foundation was Co-founded in 1978 with public health leader Larry Brilliant and humanitarian activist Wavy Gravy to treat the blinds in India, Nepal, and developing countries. It has become an international health organization.

The Love Serve Remember Foundation was organized to preserve and continue the teachings of Neem Karoli Baba and Ram Dass.

Purpose of Ashrams and Temples

Baba used to say that people are neglecting religion and service. This is going to reflect very poorly on the society. The day is not far off when these temples would remind man of God. To provide accessibility to people, Baba constructed these temples in bigger towns near the main roads.

Baba tried to fulfill the worldly desires of people to transform their heart. He made these temples such that through prayer and worship people's mundane issues were solved. The statues were infused with divine energy of Baba so they became like living deities. That is why more and more people are flocking around these temples. These temples are being recognized as holy shrines by the devotees who are increasing day by day.

These temples are neat and clean and provide peaceful silence which helps to silence the mind including those who are tourists. There is hardly anyone who does not want to visit these places to pray and stay.

The important thing to remember is that these temples and Ashrams do not have any funds or assets to make them self reliant. The expenses are increasing day by day and Baba himself is working behind the management in a subtle way. Due to his grace, the expenses are met through voluntary donations without any hassles.

Mystery of Baba

Baba remained mysterious though he worked as a normal human being. His acts were beyond imagination, and could not be reasoned out. Our mind and brain have a limitation and are unable to rationalize many things. Logic and reason have limitations. Mind cannot comprehend supernatural. True spiritual experiences can be grasped only through trust. One that is omnipotent and unlimited is beyond human comprehension through logic and reason.

One which is omnipotent is capable to do anything. His incarnation in human form and human acts is only to support his infinite powers.

Right from the beginning of creation, man has been guided by man. If God has to teach man about truth, He has to incarnate in human form. Due to parochial outlook and man's ego, there is hindrance in developing trust and love. Therefore man goes astray and unable to grasp truth. Doubt is the greatest barrier. Due to this, Baba remained a mystery for most of the people.

Baba used to say, "Those thoughts that arise in the mind and brain on account of sensory perception, cannot comprehend truth." His statement reflects the true nature of truth and proves that what is understood truth in the world is only an illusion. Baba's statement may not appear practical, but it cannot be doubted.

Our brain made of blood and flesh produces thoughts through a complex process and presents before us in a manner which appears true. Not realizing the truth we believe the product of our brain as true because we do not have any other faculty except thoughts. Since brain is part of our body, therefore it is a product of nature and world. One can learn about the body only by looking at it objectively, but it is our subjectivity. But our brain while retaining its relationship with thoughts makes decision which is not only false but also illusory.

The important point with Baba was that while he was in the human form, he was not rooted in the body. His body was a visible form of God that Hindus have described as Sat, Chit, Anand i.e. Truth, Consciousness, Bliss. It was not governed by the laws of nature but controlled nature.

Nature or Prakriti is indescribable but is recognized by the three attributes: Sattva, Rajas, and Tamas. Rajas means activity, Tamas means inertia and Sattva is the balancing power. A man is recognized according to these attributes of nature. But one who is the controller of nature or "Prakriti" cannot be known through these attributes.

Hanumanji was seen by Tulsidas as an old, dilapidated and suffering from leprosy. He was endowed with all the eight "Siddhi's" but he could not recognize him in this form.

Hanuman met Lord Rama in a Brahmin form. But he could not hide his reality before the Lord. He was capable of increasing his body or reducing it to the size of a mosquito. Tulsidas has written in the fifth episode of Ramcharit Manas called "Sunderkand" as below:

"Masak saman roop kapi dhari"

Which means Hanuman could reduce himself, to the size of a mosquito.

Further, when he encountered the demon queen "Surasa" who wanted to devour Hanuman, he enlarged his body

"जस जस सुरसा बदनु बढ़ावा। तासु दून कपि रूप देखावा॥"

"Jas Jas Surasa Badanu Badhava, Tasu Doon Kapi Roop Dikhawa"

Baba was also capable of appearing in different forms; it was difficult to recognize him. Like Hanumanji, Baba was also capable to enlarge his body or reduce it to any size.

Scientists try to investigate the material form of nature and their conclusions are based upon the physical. They are unable to penetrate deeper realities. Without effacing oneself, the truth cannot be revealed. Truth can be penetrated only by the "Siddha" who have transcended nature, not by the scientists who are confined to nature only.

Baba was capable of controlling nature. He was capable of changing nature according to his wish, water and air helped him in this. Fire would change its nature and would work as he wished. Space was always in his service. Prakriti or nature according to Hindus consists of five elements or "Bhutas": Earth, Water, Fire, Air and Space or Ether. All the five elements were in the control of Baba. Baba could disappear before the eyes of others and made others disappear. He would appear in dreams which looked real. After waking the reality would be revealed exactly as what was dreamt off. Baba would move indirectly through wind, his travel using the worldly modes would be only to prove that he was a normal human being.

His way of communication over long distances was supernatural. Baba was capable of transmitting messages and images without the use of scientific instrumentation. He was capable of blessing a childless for a child and could revive life in a dead besides removing troubles and worries. He would know the unspoken words of a visitor and could read the thoughts of a person belonging to any nation or language of the world.

Baba was truly a "Sankat Mochan." His method of removing misery of a person was unique. His methods could not be rationalized. He could take the disease of a person living anywhere upon himself. By taking the suffering upon himself he would make the person free from the disease, without his ever knowing about it. It was a common sight to see Baba surrounded by various diseases which would soon vanish without any treatment. His devotees would try to treat Baba but would not succeed because the disease was not his, but of someone else. It was difficult to know how and where his grace would descend upon someone. Sometimes, he would send a doctor without anyone's knowledge to treat a person who would soon recover through Baba's grace. It was his divine energy which could free a person from physical, mental or worldly miseries. Baba would help someone dying of untimely death. He would make a person realize the God's will and would help a person by helping him gain strength to bear the will of God by infusing confidence in him.

Baba was known as an "avatar" or incarnation of Hanuman due to his divine plays or "Lila." Hanuman Chalisa and Sunderkand were often recited for prayer by Baba's devotees. Hanuman is said to be immortal. Leaving the mortal frame of Baba is also said to be a device to become invisible from the eyes of his devotees. Even now Baba is seen either in form or in any other way through dreams and vision. He is helping even now in resolving worries of his devotees. Devotees are convinced that he is present even now in an invisible form. This is also proved by logic. He could be seen at many places at the same time, it is not difficult for him to disappear in form. The only purpose is that Baba wanted to remain away from the devotees for some time. Separation makes one understand the beloved more intensely than in form. Devotees were unable to comprehend Baba during his lifetime. They are able to feel and realize him more when he has become invisible.

Baba helped everyone from rich to poor. He did not demand anything. He worked like a common man. He was hiding his divine powers. To say that Baba was doing miracles is a wrong notion. All his deeds were real and intended to help mankind. He was not interested in attracting masses to exhibit his divine powers. To say that Baba was a "miracle Baba" would be to degrade a divine and mysterious being.

Maharaj Ji's Family

Maharaj ji was simultaneously a great Siddha Purusha Saint and a householder with a wife (who is now passed); they had 2 sons & 1 daughter & 9 grandchildren (2 boys & 7 girls most born before Babaji's Samadhi, on 9–11–73)

Maharajji's wife

Aneg Singh Sharma — Babaji's oldest son

Dharm Narain Sharma — Babaji's second son

Girija & Jagdish Bhatele Maharajji's daughter & Her husband

Maharajji's MahaSamadhi

MahaSamadhi is a saint's final Samadhi (higher state of meditation, a non-dualistic state of consciousness) of enlightenment. It is the complete absorption of consciousness in the self at the time of death. An established yogi or yogini who has attained enlightenment will pick the appropriate day and time to consciously leave their mortal body. Even though the saint is in fact leaving the physical body it shouldn't be a sad time for their devotees. Many great saints, or accomplished yogis, have said that when they leave their body they will be even more accessible to everyone. Other saints have said that after death they will be more powerful; because there won't be the restrictions of the physical body.

We can see the truth of these words by the stories we hear from people who have been touched by Maharaj ji even after his death and who have never met him in the physical form.

Neem Karoli Baba decided to leave his physical body on September 11th, 1973 in the Ramakrishna Mission hospital in Vrindavan. Baba's ashes are kept in a MahaSamadhi room at his ashram in Vrindavan. Some devotees find that sitting in this room fills them with love, and takes them deeper into meditation.

Here is a short story of one thing Maharaj ji said about MahaSamadhi:

"Maharaj ji went to Shirdi Sai Baba temple in Madras. He sat there quietly. A woman with a baby sat crying before a picture of Shirdi Sai Baba, who had left his body many years before. Maharaj ji said, "You know what she is doing?" She is asking him to cure her child, and he will do it because a guru never leaves his devotees. A guru is indestructible, immortal, and immune to old age and death."

Maharaj ji had said, "When a saint leaves his body, the temple becomes his body."

Siddhi Ma

Since the time that Maharaj ji left His body, He started manifesting more and more through Siddhi Ma's transmission. She conveyed the love that Maharaj ji is; she was an extension of that unconditional love.

Sri Siddhi Ma, a very close devotee of Maharaj-ji and considered by many to be a great yogini and saint in Her own right, left Her body on December 28, 2017. Since Maharaj-ji left His body in 1973, she blessed all of his ashrams with her compassionate guiding presence. For about 44 years, she continued Maharaj-Ji's work of comforting souls and made sure that His ashrams and temples are immaculate seats for His powerful divine presence.

Maharaj ji had said, "When a saint leaves his body, the temple becomes his body."

2
Spiritual Practices in India and the Role of Neem Karoli Baba

"मय्यावेश्य मनो ये मां नित्ययुक्ता उपासते।
श्रद्धया परयोपेतास्ते में युक्ततमा मताः।।"

"The Blessed Lord said: Those who fix their minds on me and always engage in my devotion with steadfast faith, I consider them to be the best yogis."

-----*Srimad Bhagvat Gita Ch 12 verse 2*

"(अगुन सगुन दुइ ब्रह्म. सरूपा। अकथ अगाध अनादि अनूपा॥)"

"It is the devotion (Bhakti) of the devotee that forces the Nirguna Brahman which is quality-less, formless, invisible and unborn, to become Saguna Brahman with qualities."

Ram Charit Manas

This book is not a book of philosophy or religion. It is written primarily for the purpose of resolving worries and anxieties that haunt man from time to time and eat away our energy.

This book is a guide book to infuse confidence amongst those who have lost all hopes. My purpose would be solved if this helps to resolve worries of a troubled soul.

I was a student of Science. I had studied Einstein's theory of relativity. I used to ask my professor of Physics one important question; that often gripped my mind. I wanted to know if everything was relative in the universe; there must be a reference absolute point with respect to which all matter, space and time were relative. My professor could not satisfy me; he said "Such questions are outside the scope of Science."

I began looking elsewhere for answers. I became interested in religions.

In Hinduism, this absolute is called "God" or "Soul" or the "Atman" or "Brahma." This was the source from where everything in the universe emanated. In Buddhism, it is called axle of a wheel. The wheel is "Samsara" or universe and the "Axle" around which everything moves is the centre of the universe. Without the axle, the wheel cannot move. Science could analyse only the universe and its laws but not the axle. That is why my professor of Physics could not satisfy me. It was beyond the scope of science.

Buddha's Dharma chakra (Wheel)   Indian Flag with wheel

Above picture shows Buddhist wheel of "Samsara" and the "Axle" around which everything moves.

India accepted the wheel of the Buddhism on the national flag and various emblems. Although Hinduism called the centre as "Atman,"

Buddha called it "Anatta" or "Shunyata" which means nothingness. The Ashoka Chakra is a depiction of the dharma chakra; represented with 24 spokes.

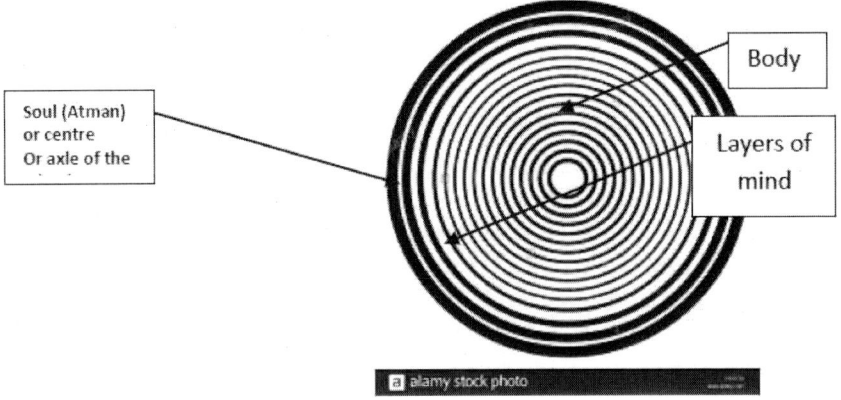

Above picture shows the periphery and the centre in another way. The outermost periphery is the body. Within this there are a number of concentric circles that represent different layers of the mind, conscious, subconscious, unconscious etc. To reach to the axle or the Atman one has to penetrate within from body to various layers of mind before one can reach to the centre.

The purpose of all the masters who were born on this planet was to make man centered in his being (on the axle) for a blissful living. A true religion is one that makes man centered on the non-moving axle. In times of anxiety, worry and frustration we lose our centre, we are off-centered, moving on the wheel which is changing all the time. It is never constant. Worry, anxiety, misery are changing all the time.

When Buddha, through his meditation, stumbled upon the axle, he became enlightened.

Different spiritual practices that developed in various cultures were intended to take man out of worries and anxieties and provide support to come to the axle, sublimate and come out of the negativity to move towards positivity until one reaches the divinity within, i.e. the absolute.

But the spiritual practices change with time. What was applicable during the age of Upanishads or during the times of Patanjali, Krishna, Buddha, and Mahavira no longer applies in this age of "Kali Yug." With each Yuga or epoch according to Hinduism, the negative energies on this planet go up. Therefore the techniques and practices of ancient times won't work now. New methods have to be devised. Neem Karoli Baba has helped mankind to look for ways that are applicable in modern age.

I would like to discuss about the different spiritual practices in India and how Neem Karoli Baba has been contributing to raising human consciousness on this planet through devotion and prayer.

This book is primarily intended to introduce the Hindu way of looking at spirituality to a western reader.

Earth is the third planet from the Sun and the only astronomical object known to harbor life. According to various sources of evidence, Earth formed over 4.5 billion years ago.

Within the first billion years of Earth's history, life appeared in the oceans. Subsequently, other life forms developed until man came to inhabit this planet. With the passage of time, man was becoming aware about the surroundings. He became inquisitive to know about the world of objects around him. That is how the primary inquiry must have begun.

Further inquiry must have developed when man started penetrating within himself. Thoughts and feelings also became the subject of inquiry because these were driving him into pleasure and pain, misery and sorrow.

Birth and death must have also become the subject of inquiry.

Man must have come to realize that there were objects perceptible to the senses but there were also other supernatural powers in existence not graspable by human senses.

Such things began to be regarded as divine due to their transcendental origins or because their attributes or qualities were superior to things of the earth. Divine things were regarded as eternal and based in truth, while material things were regarded as ephemeral and based in illusion.

The search for such supernatural powers led to various religions throughout the world in different lands and cultures.

We can broadly divide religions into two categories viz those that developed in the west and those that developed in the east.

Judaism, Christianity and Islam developed in the west. Hinduism, Buddhism, Jainism, Sikhism developed in the east. Besides, there also developed some other religions in different parts of the world based upon certain other beliefs.

Hinduism, Buddhism, Jainism, Sikhism developed in India.

All the religions that developed in India differ in many things but all agree on one point i.e. reincarnation.

As against this, the religions in the west don't believe in afterlife.

Everywhere in the world there is a concept of God in one way or the other. What is God? Is it a concept of man? Is there someone high up in the sky watching us? Why does man suffer? How to come out of anxiety, worry and fear of uncertainty?

These are some questions that have haunted man since time immemorial to discover truth. Is reality only that is seen or is there something unseen which also governs the universe?

God was an invention of man. It must have been invented primarily because of fear. Man was helpless. He was capable of doing many things but there were many things beyond his control. Man was product of nature and so was all life. Hindus call nature as "Prakriti." The Sankhya philosophy of Hinduism is based on "Prakriti" and "Purusha" and is the most scientific explanation to understand spirituality.

Nowhere in the world have so many experiments been done as in India for religious enquiry. India has never been dogmatic. It has always opened new doors for exploration in the inner word. What India lacks is exploration in the outer world through science. That has been the cause of poverty in India which is appalling.

On the contrary, the west has concentrated on exploration in the outer world (the periphery). It did not explore within. That has made both the East and the West lopsided.

We need a world today where inner and outer exploration goes hand in hand to make the world a holy place. It has become unholy.

People from the West often come to India in search of a Guru. What is a Guru? A Guru is a middleman between man and God. Man needs support of someone to resolve his worries. That is how priesthood came into existence. A Guru is a consultant. But contrary to the western professional counselors, Indian Gurus have no qualification or certification. Anybody can engage himself in some kind of spiritual practice and can call himself a Guru.

A true master is that who has experienced divinity. There mere presence emanates energy where one can bathe in silence. But such masters are very rare and do not publicize.

Westerners are not aware that there are false gurus and true gurus. They are unable to discriminate. Thus they fall prey to many false gurus. There cannot be a standardization or certification in this area because it concerns invisible product and services. There can be no quality assurance until one accidentally stumbles upon a true master.

Those who came to Neem Karoli Baba from the west stumbled upon him accidentally without any prior knowledge about him. Baba was completely against any kind of publicity around him. But those who stumbled upon him were transformed. They became devotees of Baba. Baba never made disciples.

This was a miracle. Miracles happen.

A westerner, visiting India, fails to understand different spiritual practices prevalent in India.

I would therefore like to provide a brief account about the spiritual practices in India for the benefit of readers from the west.

As mentioned earlier, I am neither an expert in philosophy nor in religion but have definitely travelled in different paths to develop my understanding until I stumbled upon Neem Karoli Baba. I never saw him physically, never went to his ashram, have been bedridden with a deadly disease but am deriving energy to write this book from my heart.

There are so many different paths in India that one is likely to get confused. The western religions are not so confusing because there is a clear cut concept of one God, one prophet and a holy book or scripture.

On the contrary, in Hinduism, there are many scriptures, many deities, and even a formless God which complicates understanding the religion.

There are ways where no God in form is needed, and ways where God in form is needed.

As I said before, the aim of spirituality is to lead a life free of worry, anxiety and misery. This is called "Bliss" or "Anand." Misery or anxiety is a product of human mind. Animals don't suffer because they are not conscious the same way as man is.

Mind has been explored by the western psychology and also in India by seers like Patanjali. That part of the mind which is engaged in thinking is called the conscious mind. The other part of the mind which is engaged in feeling is called the subconscious mind. Deeper than these is the unconscious layer of the mind which is under the control of nature to perform essential activities like breathing, digestion, sex etc. These cannot be willed by man.

Based on these three layers of the mind, different religious practices were evolved in India.

Nirgun Upasana (Worship of God without a form):

Nirgun Upasana deals with the thinking layer of the mind, which in modern psychology is called the "Conscious mind."

It is presumed that it is the thinking mind which is the cause of worry and anxiety.

This spiritual practice to silence the thinking mind is called meditation. It is to train the mind in such a way that one is able to watch thoughts (good and bad) without identification. The basic premise is that through identification of thoughts in the conscious mind, anxiety, worry and miseries arise.

There are thousands of ways to practice meditation in India. But it is difficult. In times of crisis, the thoughts overtake human mind and man becomes a victim. Depression follows.

The practice where no God in form is needed is called "Nirgun Upasana." "Nirgun" means without attributes.

Buddha denied God. Mahavira denied God. Atheism is also considered a valid path to spirituality. God can manifest in several forms with "no form" being one of them. Charvakas, Sankhya, Mimamsa, Vedanta, and other schools of Hinduism deny existence of any God with form. But this path is considered difficult to follow.

God is formless. It is without a name and form. Hindus name the formless God as "Brahman" or "Parmatman."

"Brahman" is the primordial reality that creates, maintains and withdraws within it the universe. It is the "ultimate that is the cause of everything including all gods," the divine being, Lord, distinct God, or God within oneself"

The Upanishads which are ancient most scriptures say "*अहं ब्रह्म अस्मि*" *"aham brahmāsmi"* or *"I am Brahman."*

Above statement of the Upanishads is a conclusion after one has attained a state of watchfulness of mind. It is a result of spiritual practice, a declaration. But many people repeat these words unknowingly and write books and treatises. They mislead.

Brahman is the ultimate "eternally constant" reality, while the observed universe is a different kind of reality but one which is "temporary, changing" called "Maya" in various orthodox Hindu schools. "Maya" in Hinduism is the same thing as "Samsar" in Buddhism. Maya pre-exists and co-exists with Brahman—the Ultimate Reality, the Highest Universal, the Cosmic Principle.

Nirguna Brahman—the Brahman without attributes, is the Brahman as it really is. "Brahman" in Hinduism, and "Axle" of the wheel in Buddhism, mean the same thing.

Brahman and Maya are the basic realities in Nirgun Upasana.

Brahman is freedom. Maya is slavery. Man comes out of God but becomes a slave to his instincts in this world. That slavery causes misery. To be free of Maya is the aim of Indian spirituality. Then only one can be free of desires, attachments and Maya. This is Yoga. Yoga means union with God.

But unfortunately, even Yoga is being propagated wrongly around the world.

United Nations has declared 21st June as International Yoga day each year to propagate Yoga. But it is unfortunate that this Yoga is related only to the physical body and some "Asana" or postures for body fitness. This is not Yoga.

In India some Yoga Gurus have gained international popularity by teaching Yogasanas for physical fitness. That is taking the masses into a wrong direction. It is good to keep the body fit but that is not enough.

Yoga means freedom from Maya and union with God.

Maharshi Patanjali compiled "Yoga Sutras" in eight steps. Each step has to be practiced. But these are difficult to practice and are not suitable for the modern age. Man has changed since the times of Patanjali.

Māyā pre-exists and co-exists with Brahman – the Ultimate Principle, Pure Consciousness. Maya is perceived reality, one that does not reveal the hidden principles, the true reality. Maya is unconscious, Atman is conscious.

Maya is born, changes, evolves, dies with time, from circumstances, due to invisible principles of nature, states the Upanishads.

Atman-Brahman is eternal, unchanging, invisible principle, unaffected absolute and resplendent consciousness. Maya concept in the Upanishads, is pre-existing with Brahman, just like the possibility of a future tree pre-exists in the seed of the tree.

Mediation or Yoga is the path of attainment of Brahman by growing awareness, watchfulness and observation without thinking. There is no need to have a God in form. It is the path of will.

Meditation is a way to reach impersonal God.

Meditation can be best described in Zen haiku by Basho:

> *'Sitting silently,*
>
> *Doing nothing,*
>
> *The spring comes*
>
> *And the grass grows by itself.'*

Meditation is a simple process, of watching your own mind. Not fighting with the mind, not trying to control it either, just remaining there, a choice less witness.

The method to reach the Impersonal God is meditation. This does not require a god in form. Buddha taught meditation techniques. Patanjali in his Yoga Sutras discusses about eight fold way to transcend mind into "Samadhi." Osho devised many meditation techniques to transcend mind for the modern man. He spoke extensively on 112 techniques of Shiva for meditation.

Osho's methods are based on cleansing of repressed feelings through cathartic processes. There are many other techniques that he devised for the modern man to become a witness to watchfulness, awareness without identification of thoughts. But as I said earlier, these are difficult in times of crisis.

On the contrary, J. Krishnamurti was against Gurus. He wanted man to walk alone without the support of any Guru or god in form. He was an adept in Hindu "Sankhya Philosophy" which means pure knowledge or understanding without any spiritual practices.

To what extent these methods have proved successful is a matter of research.

Sagun Upasana (Worship of God with a Form)

Contrary to the Nirgun Upasana, there is "Sagun Upasana" where God is seen in form with attributes or "Gunas."

This method deals with the sub-conscious layer of the mind which is the feeling part, contrary to the thinking part of the conscious mind.

Feeling comes in the heart, thinking comes in the mind.

Hindus have divided three layers of existence of human mind; thinking, feeling and being. This is also called body, mind and soul.

The goal is to reach to the being. One can start from the thinking mind that is meditation.

One can also start from the feeling mind; that is prayer.

Finally, one reaches the being part that is universal.

"Sagun Upasana" is the path of devotion or prayer.

A personal God in form is the basis of "Sagun Upasana."

Heart is closer to the being than mind.

For prayer no techniques are required as in meditative practices.

In India, God with form has infinite attributes.

Hinduism conceives of the trinity of Gods based on the principles of creation, sustenance and destruction.

"Brahma" is the creator, "Vishnu" is the sustainer and "Shiva" is the destroyer.

"Brahma" the creator, "Vishnu" the sustainer and "Shiva" the destroyer

All schools of "Vaishnavism" accept Narayana, or Krishna, or Vishnu as the Sagun Brahman.

Shiva is the Saguna Brahman of "Shaivism."

Goddess Shakti or Parvati, Durga, Kali, Mahalakshmi, or Gayatri is seen as the Saguna Brahman in Shaktism.

There are many deities, gods and goddesses for worship and one has to develop trust in a personal god called the "Isht Devata." Chanting Mantra and invocation is the foundation of prayer.

In India, a deity is called "Devata." "Devata" means that which gives life energy called "Prana." "Prana" is the life energy. During death "Prana" leaves the physical body. Yoga has talked about five bodies in humans. The physical body which is the grossest is called "Anna Maya Kosha" or the body produced by food. The second body behind "Annamaya Kosha" is subtler than the first body and is called "Prana Sharir" or the etheric body. This subtle body can be detected now through scientific instruments using electro photonic imaging called "Kirlian photography."

Worship and prayer are means to grow Prana body. In misery and sorrow Prana reduces whereas in prayer and devotion Prana expands.

In a temple in India, a deity or God in stone is first established and then through rituals and mantras it is made conscious or "prana" is infused. This is known as "Prana Pratishtha." The god in statue then becomes alive. He is then worshipped as if it is a living being higher in spirit. It is washed, cleaned, sprayed with scented water and flowers, given eatables as "Bhog" which is then distributed to devotees as "Prasad." "Prasad" also means grace. The temple is closed for god or deity to retire, and then woken up at sunrise with pleasantries, washing, offering of fresh clothes, food and interaction with the devotees. The temple, with chanting and prayer then becomes a place to raise the energy level.

The purpose of spirituality is to reach to a state of blissfulness or pure love so as to reach divinity either without a god in form or with the support of a "Devi" or "Devata." Devi is the female consort of a Devata. There is no concept of a female god in western religions. But in India every God has a female consort.

Saraswati, the Hindu goddess of knowledge, music, arts, wisdom and learning is the consort of Brahma. Lakshmi Hindu goddess of wealth, fortune, and prosperity (both material and spiritual) is the consort and active energy of Vishnu. Parvati is the wife of Shiva – the destroyer, recycler and regenerator of universe and all life. She is the mother of Hindu gods Ganesh and Karttikeya.

Devi Lakshmi, Devi Durga and Devi Saraswati

Hindus have also worshiped sun, moon, trees, rivers etc because these also give us life or Prana. Without sun there would be no life. Therefore, everything that is life – giving is worshipped by Hindus. Sun is also a devata and worshipped as such.

River worship   Tree Worship

Pilgrims bathing in the Holy River in Kumbha Mela

Sun Worship

Moon Worship

With the scientific development, doubt has grown, trust is disappearing and worship is becoming only a ritual. That is the cause of deforestation, environmental degradation and destruction of life on this planet.

Devata symbolizes higher form of consciousness. Deities help humans to grow consciousness and be blissful.

Prayer and worship is an expression of gratitude to everything that is life – giving. Without gratitude, prayer is not possible; it would simply remain a ritual. In India life in every form was a subject of worship including animals, birds and plants. Non-violence or "Ahimsa" was not just a philosophy, it was a holistic approach to ecology because everything was considered interconnected and interrelated with each other. If we destroy a tree, we are indirectly destroying ourselves. We are all connected with each other, plants, birds, animals, sun, moon, and river; air, space, earth in short, everything surrounding us animate and inanimate.

With the passage of time, several cults developed in India for worship through rituals. The spirit of prayer and devotion is lost if it becomes a cult. Cults kill the spirit of religion and promote fanaticism. Prayer becomes less devotional and more of a tradition.

Misery is a human phenomenon. It comes with the evolution of mind. Animals, birds, plants and other species do not have a developed mind and therefore do not suffer from worry, anxiety and misery. With mind comes time, past and future, which brings anxiety.

Unless man can transcend mind and go beyond mind he cannot come out of misery. Meditation and Prayer are two ways to transcend mind. Meditation does not need support of a God in form. Prayer needs support of a God in form. Out of these two paths, meditation is difficult. Those who can be in love with a divine energy, with devotion and trust, can easily come out of troubles created by the thinking mind.

I was also on the path of meditation for almost 40 years. But I was in sorrow and misery due to various circumstances in my life. I had no faith in prayer and devotion and did not go to any temple throughout my life. I was an atheist, an agnostic and travelled the path of Buddha for meditation. I do not deny that one can arrive through meditation. But it is difficult. In situations when one is hopeless in life, he needs support.

Buddha Meditating

Buddha denied God. He was not in favor of creating a statue. He did not promote idol worship. He was not accepted in India. His following in India is negligible (0.8%). Buddhism spread throughout Asia except in India. However, Buddha's disciples or Bhikkus could not remain without a personal God. They started worshipping Buddha as God. Buddha's statues were built around the world for worship even though Buddha had denied it. The Bhikkhus started worshipping and prayed "Buddham Sharanam Gacchami."

Osho Dynamic Meditation

Osho Nadbrahma Meditation

Islam is also against idol worship. In India, many statues of Indian Gods and temples were destroyed during Muslim invasion. But Muslims also go to pray in a mosque in the direction of their holy shrine towards Mecca. Kaaba is an idol (black stone) worshipped by Muslims.

The point that I want to emphasize is that man cannot conceive of a God without form.

Buddhism, Islam, Christianity and other organized religions have now become cults. The Masters of these religions came to share their love and divine energy. But their followers created organized religions around the masters. The preaching's of these masters were converted into scriptures which created cults or "Ism." Prayer cannot work through organized religion, scriptures or "Ism." One is compelled to become part of an organized religion by birth and not by any devotion.

Jesus and his 12 apostles

This is not devotion. True devotion cannot be taught, it has to be caught.

An organized religion requires belief in a God, a prophet or son of God and a holy scripture.

Belief is not trust. Belief system is established through tradition. Trust is individual and belongs to the realm of heart.

As science progressed on this planet, it has brought more misery. Science is a product of a developed mind. It does not know anything about heart, love and divinity. Science has made life to move away from heart to head. For devotion and prayer one has to move from head to heart. Mind is logical, heart transcends logic.

Rama, Hanuman and other deities are mythological gods. Their history is not much known.

In India, instead of history, "Puranas" were written to convey mythological stories for inner exploration. Vedas, Upanishads, Puranas and epics were meant to convey divine experiences by the seers.

Mythology is not fiction. It is also not a fact. But mythologies convey the truth.

Logic and reason are based upon facts grasped through our senses. It does not support anything that is beyond senses.

I was also a non-believer throughout my life. I never believed in the power of prayers and devotion. I was on the path of "Gyan Yoga."

In India, God is defined as having three attributes: "Satyam, Shivam, Sundaram," which means "Truth, Goodness and Beauty."

Truth can be attained in many ways but primarily there are three approaches in Indian yoga.

These are: Gyan Yoga, Karma Yoga and Bhakti Yoga.

Yoga means "Union," union with God. Patanjali describes Yoga as cessation of mind. Once the mind ceases, union with divine happens.

Gyan Yoga corresponds to truth or Satyam. It is the path of knowledge. To know the reality as it is, not through thinking but to know it as it is. Thinking distorts the reality.

Karma Yoga corresponds to Shivam or Goodness. It is the path of selfless service. Shivam means virtue. Shivam means living in action. Whatever a mystic does is Shivam. Neem Karoli Baba believed in action. He did not deliver discourses.

Bhakti Yoga corresponds to Sundaram or Beauty. Bhakti Yoga is devotion towards a personal god. Receptivity to divine is an experience of Sundaram. Those who are receptive to the divine energy are the true seekers. Hanuman is a devotee of Rama.

According to Hinduism, all life has come out of God and would ultimately go back to God, the source.

Until life merges with the source, which is God, man would suffer through the cycle of birth and death.

All the religions in the world discuss about creation and how God created the universe. In India, God was conceived not as a person or form; it was formless, as creativity, the source of all energy.

But as I have said earlier, man needs a God in form for prayer and worship. Several Gods in various forms gradually developed for worship and prayer.

Through prayer, worship and surrender one can get rid of worries. Surrender means total trust. Surrender your worries to a God with total trust. And the miracle happens. That is the story of Neem Karoli Baba. Those who surrender their worries to Hanuman with total trust are taken care of by Hanuman. Hanuman and Neem Karoli Baba mean one and the same thing.

Consciousness

Life on this planet evolved from rocks to man. In this process of evolution consciousness has evolved. Rocks are unconscious, man is partially conscious, a Buddha is fully conscious.

Man has become conscious through collective evolution by nature.

But this consciousness is only tip of the iceberg. A large part still remains unconscious.

Due to this partial evolution of consciousness, man suffers. With a fully evolved consciousness there is no misery, no sorrow. Life is blissful, compassionate and full of love.

Conscious mind is the thinking mind.

Due to the thinking process of the conscious mind, time is created. Past and future is created. Memory and imagination is created. This eats away energy or Prana. Involuntary thinking is the root cause of all worries.

Through Kirlian photography it is now possible to detect energy level in the subtle body by "Aura" reading and to see how negative thoughts affect the Prana energy. Through meditation and prayer the Prana energy grows and makes one healthy and the effect can be seen through Kirlian photography. The thinking process reduces prana whereas silence brought out through meditation and prayer grows prana energy.

Energies endowed by nature such as sex, anger, lust, attachment, fear etc for survival purposes are raw energies. These energies are given by nature for survival purposes. Man can transcend nature and transform nature's energies into divine energies through meditation, chanting and prayers.

Sex is the basic energy given to plants, birds, animals and humans for survival of the species. Except man no other species is sex obsessed. Sex is a natural phenomenon for species other than man. Only man is obsessed with sex. Man has become unnatural. Through meditation and prayer the sex energy in man is transformed into love, a divine energy. Therefore man can transcend nature and become divine which is not possible in any other lower life forms. Man can also fall below animal.

Through transformation of nature's energies sex becomes love, anger becomes compassion.

God is the source of all energies. By transforming these energies into divine energies one is purified and reaches to the source which is formless.

But to go straight to the formless is difficult, therefore a twofold process of prayer has been devised, the first step being that of prayer through a god in form and the second step from form to formless.

In Bible it is said that "in the beginning God created the heaven and the earth. And the earth was without form, and void; and darkness was upon the face of the deep. And the Spirit of God moved upon the face of the waters. And God said, "Let there be light: and there was light."

This is a mythology to convey the truth. It is neither fiction nor fact.

Light is the basic energy which is not derived from any other source except God. All other energies are derived from Light. And God is the source of light energy which is the purest energy. By God is meant all that exists and also that which is non-existent (or invisible to the senses).

Without light there cannot be any life.

Light is the source of all life.

Life evolves from lower to higher forms.

And life when fully evolved becomes love or divine.

Light, life and love are three stages of evolution. Light evolves from God, life evolves from light, and life evolves into love which again becomes God. Then the circle is complete.

Without light there can be no life. Love is the culmination of life. God is the source of light and life. Through evolutionary process we go back ultimately to the source. Until we go back to the source, the evolutionary process continues. This is the Indian way of interpreting God and life.

Before divine love happens one has to pass through miseries in life. Misery gives an opportunity to search for a divine support of God. Until that misery is encountered, one lives in hope. Misery means hopelessness.

The statement "God is love" is a declaration of a fully evolved being be it Jesus, Mohammed, Krishna, Rama, Buddha or others. The human love is a duality between love and hate, the divine love that Jesus talks about is non-dual. It is pure love.

The fall of Adam and Eve in the biblical story is the symbol of life coming to earth from the Garden of Eden. It is the story of evolution of life. Finally life becomes love or God. Life comes out of God and goes back to God. It is then a full circle. Prior to that, one passes through sufferings.

Neem Karoli Baba showered his love to whosoever came to him. He was love personified. This love was divine unlike human love which is both love and hate.

Facts are experiences graspable through human senses. Truth is beyond sensory perception. One accepts that there is much more beyond senses. There is a world that cannot be seen but can be experienced. Only those who accept both the seen and the unseen, one day stumble upon truth.

Their experiences are, however, individual. Science only accepts facts. Facts can be verified, reproduced and repeated. True religion is experiential, individual and cannot be verified, and proved. Such experiences are individual and therefore mystical.

Doubt is essential for Science to explore the outer world. On the contrary, trust is the base for inner exploration. Since human mind is oriented only to sensory perceptions, it denies all that is beyond senses. Mind distrusts.

What Lord said in the holy Bible cannot be proved by scientific facts. But it is a truth conveyed in the Holy Scripture for the purpose of growth in the human consciousness. With the development of Science, miracles performed by Jesus have also become a matter of doubt for the modern age man. The miracles performed by Neem Karoli Baba in recent times have been recorded by his devotees only to establish the truth. There are theologians, who deny the biblical stories about miracles performed by Jesus. Science creates doubt, religion is based on trust.

In Indian mythology gods and deities do not demand any proof but are a means for realization. These mythologies are meant to develop trust in divine powers.

Meditation and Prayer

I would like to briefly discuss the purpose of meditation and prayer. On this planet, only man meditates or prays. No other species need meditation or prayer. Why? Because, except man other life forms on this planet do not have a developed mind and do not suffer.

What happens with the evolution of mind?

A human child when born does not have a developed mind. He is born an animal.

As the human child grows, he is taught to learn alphabets, words, language to communicate. Without this, the human child would remain like any other beast and may die prematurely. With alphabets, words and language the child learns to identify and associate objects and persons to survive in the world.

With this learning of communication, thought, memory and imagination are created.

Thought, memory, imaginations are part of the mind. Conscious mind is only a tip of the total mind. It thinks. Below the conscious mind there are deeper layers of mind called the sub-conscious, unconscious, collective unconscious and cosmic unconscious mind. In the west Jung explored the deeper layers of mind, beyond the unconscious mind. The unconscious mind was first explored by the famous psychologist Sigmund Freud.

Conscious mind is used when faced with real problems for survival in the world during the waking time. In a life threatening real situation, "fight" and "flight" instincts given by nature for survival become activated.

But when this thinking of the conscious mind, in other than real life situations, becomes involuntary, mind becomes a chatterbox. It starts brooding over past and future which creates worry, anxiety and suffering. This thinking becomes involuntary and habitual. It brings negative thoughts in the mind which creates depression and kills. Negative thoughts are the cause of several physical diseases.

The purpose of all spiritual practices whether meditation or prayer is to grow more and more silence within, to master the thinking mind and to grow consciousness beyond the thinking conscious mind.

Conscious mind evolved in man through the collective natural process. Once the conscious mind evolved, the role of nature came to an end.

This partial development of the conscious mind has created all the misery in man. Man fears about the future uncertainties in life. Money was invented for security. Man works hard to accumulate wealth, to secure him. Thinking mind is the cause of all the worry and anxiety.

Unless man grows consciousness beyond the thinking mind, he shall remain in misery.

Nature would not be of any help for further growth of consciousness; it has to be an individual choice. Meditation and Prayer are ways to grow consciousness in order to come out of worry, anxiety and hopeless life situations. One has to go beyond the thinking mind.

In prayer, support of a divine energy is required to get rid of anxiety and worry produced by thoughts in the conscious mind. With the support of divine energy the negativity transforms into higher level.

Hindu Prayer

In meditation, one does not need any external support. It is the result of individual effort and is therefore difficult.

Meditation is an effort through will. Devotion is through surrender to a god.

Meditation is like sailing in water through a boat by rowing it oneself. One has to paddle the boat all by himself.

Prayer is like sailing in water on a boat through a mast and anchor. It is an effortless boating through the wind.

I would like to clarify this by a story.

A cow went into a forest to graze grass. By the evening she saw a tiger slowly moving towards her. Fearing the tiger she started running away.

The tiger also ran after her.

The cow saw a pond nearby. She jumped into the pond.

The tiger also followed and jumped into the pond.

The pond was not very deep but the water was muddy.

The distance between the cow and the tiger reduced.

The cow started sinking in the muddy water.

The tiger too started sinking, and despite closeness to the cow could not catch hold her. Both started sinking knee deep and could not move any further.

After sometime the cow asked the tiger, "Do you have any master?"

The tiger growled and said "I am master of the jungle, no one is my master."

The cow said, "But what use is of your energy"?

The tiger said to the cow, "You too are about to die, you are also like me."

The cow smiled and said, "When my master would go home in the evening and would not find me, he would start searching for me and would take me out of this muddy water."

A little while later, the master of the cow came, took the cow out of the mud, and brought it home

While returning both the cow and her master looked at each other with gratitude. The master wanted to rescue the tiger also but could not do so because it was dangerous.

Cow is the symbol of a surrendered heart. Tiger is the symbol of an egoist. Master is the symbol of a "Sat Guru."

One always needs a support of a friend, a Guru or an empathetic person.

As already mentioned, even those who practice meditation have taken support of a form.

This book is primarily a story of support through devotion and prayer.

In prayer, one has to relinquish the doubting conscious mind and enter into the trusting subconscious mind.

The subconscious mind has been researched widely in psychology and is used for hypnotherapy. In hypnotherapy, an induced sleep is created so that the conscious mind (doubting mind) goes to sleep. Thereafter the hypnotherapist gets access to the subconscious mind which is open to suggestion and does not doubt. A trust arises in the sub conscious mind and the suggestion works. Hypnotherapy is thereupatic. Trust works.

I also learnt Hypnotherapy and was able to help many who were facing difficulties because of various obsessions. I took my clients even to their past lives to get rid of issues that were troubling them because of some happenings in previous lives.

Hypnotherapy is not meditation. Meditation is deeper than the subconscious mind.

Similarly, in prayer the doubting mind has to be bypassed and access has to be gained into the trusting subconscious mind. A divine deity helps to raise our energy during prayer and chanting which works through imagination in the sub-conscious mind. In the subconscious mind there is no difference between imagination and reality. Once the seeds of prayer are sown, it helps us to elevate our energy and we feel blessed and ecstatic. We surrender our will to the will of a god. By surrendering our will we are free. In India, it is said that through "Bhakti" or devotion we acquire "Shakti" or energy and through "Shakti" we become free or reach to a stage called "Mukti." "Shakti," "Bhakti" and "Mukti" is a growth process beginning with "Bhakti" or devotion or surrender.

I wish to tell a story to clarify the purpose of surrender.

A monk boarded a train. He sat in a third class compartment. He put his box on his head.

The other passengers said, "What are you doing? Put your luggage down on the floor and sit comfortably."

The monk said, "I have purchased a ticket only for myself, so I was thinking that to put more weight on the train will be wrong. So I am keeping the weight on my head."

They said, "Have you gone mad? Even if you keep the weight on your head, the weight will be on the train, so why are you putting weight on your head unnecessarily? Keep it on the floor and sit comfortably. The train is bound to carry the weight whether you put it on your head or on the floor."

The monk said, "I thought there were ignorant people on the train but now I see that there are wise people here."

They said "We don't understand what you mean."

Then the monk said, "In life I have seen everybody carrying their burdens on their heads, the weight of which could have been left to existence or God. I have seen everyone carrying the burden of their anxieties on their heads-mountains and mountains of worries that could be left to God; God would have carried it. I thought that all of you in this compartment might get angry so I kept the luggage on my head. But you are wise enough…"

They said "We are only wise in this compartment. We are all riding on life's train, but we keep the entire burden on our heads. We keep it on our heads, because who else's' head shall we keep it on?"

In devotion and prayer to a god, burden is not to be kept on one's head. It should be surrendered to a god or deity. Then one is free from all anxiety.

Neem Karoli Baba said, "Why unnecessarily worry, while I am there."

Surrender your worries to the god, trust him and he shall make you free from worries.

I have tried to briefly explain prayer and devotion through modern psychology in terms of various layers of mind.

Man lives at three levels: Thinking, feeling and being.

Through food we create bio-energy. This bio-energy creates thinking.

If we starve, we lose energy and our thinking also starts diminishing.

But below thinking there is another layer of feeling.

Rene Descartes the western philosopher believed only in the thinking mind. He said, "Cogito, Ergo, Sum" meaning thereby "I think therefore I am." He was a thinker, a philosopher, a mathematician. For a philosopher, thinker and mathematician only the thinking mind exists. He does not know the deeper layers of heart and feeling. Descartes did not discuss anything about heart and feeling. He is founder of scientific thinking in the west. With the development of science in the West, thinking became predominant. For the western mind only intellect is supreme. That is the cause of anxiety, worry and misery in the West. Even the East has now been influenced by the western mind. It is now a global society, the distinction between east and west has been lost.

Thoughts and feelings are energies and vibrations at different frequencies. Thoughts are gross vibrations, feelings are subtle vibrations. Divine energies are even subtler vibrations.

These vibrations can be measured today by scientific instruments. Beta, Alpha, Theta and Delta waves are produced by thought waves and can be measured. One who lives only in the thinking mind produces Beta waves which are the grossest and eat away our energy. Alpha and theta waves are produced in the sub conscious mind during hypnosis, meditation and prayer. Delta waves are the subtlest and produced in deep meditative states.

We can all feel vibrations. If we are around a person with negative thoughts we can feel the vibes. Thoughts are like things.

The "Prana" energy is sucked if we are around a person having negativity.

Music is a subtle vibration which takes us into silence.

I am talking of the music that developed in India through meditation and prayer in the temples and not the western pop music.

The structure of a temple, the dome was also designed to create sounds that helped to silence the mind and raise our energy level.

Prayer with devotion takes us into deeper layers where subtle vibrations can be experienced.

Anyone who has been with enlightened masters can feel the energy vibrations if he is tuned to feel subtle energies.

Incarnations

What is incarnation, and why enlightened beings visit this planet in human form from time to time?

Krishna in the Gita says:

यदा यदा हि धर्मस्य ग्लानिर्भवति भारत।
अभ्युत्थानमधर्मस्य तदात्मानं सृजाम्यहम्॥ ४/७
परित्राणाय साधूनां विनाशाय च दुष्कृताम्।
धर्मसंस्थापनार्थाय संभवामि युगे युगे॥ ४/८

> *"Whenever there is decay of righteousness, O Bharata,*
> *And there is exaltation of unrighteousness, then I myself come forth;*
> *For the protection of the good, for the destruction of evil-doers,*
> *For the sake of firmly establishing righteousness, I am born*
> *from age to age."*

Similarly, Goswami Tulsidas in Ram Charit Manas says:

> "जब-जब होई धरम के हानि...!
> बढ़हिं अधम असुर अभिमानी...!!
> तब-तब प्रभु धर विविध शरीरा...!
> हरहिं कृपानिधि सज्जन पीरा......!!"

> *"That is, when sin increases, then there is a need for God to*
> *come to the defense of religion"*

The above verses describe about the purpose of divine energies descending on this planet.

In Hinduism, incarnations are divine spirits coming to this planet in human form for the purpose of raising consciousness and to overcome evil spirits from dominating the planet. The concept of incarnation or "Avatar" is in the "Sagun Upasana." It does not exist in "Nirgun Upasana."

In India, all the incarnations are of Lord Vishnu. The first incarnation was fish in the ocean.

As life evolved further, consciousness grew. Man became conscious. But a large part of human mind still remained unconscious. This is also supported by modern theories in Psychology from Sigmund Freud onwards.

As consciousness grew, life evolved further. Incarnations of Rama and Krishna are human forms of fully evolved spirits.

Brahma, Vishnu and Mahesh (Shiva) are the trinity of Indian gods depicting life created by Brahma, sustained by Vishnu and destroyed by Shiva.

Rama and Hanuman are divine incarnations. Rama is incarnation of Vishnu, whereas Hanuman is partial incarnation of Shiva. Incarnation means fully evolved spirits coming to earth in a body with divine energy to help man grow into consciousness.

I do not wish to dwell upon the mythological stories about various incarnations. But I wish to emphasize that these are neither fiction nor facts. But these mythologies convey some truth which can be experienced though not proved. Fall of Adam and Eve is also a mythological story to indicate a truth. It is neither fiction nor fact.

God incarnates in human form on this planet from time to time. In Hinduism, in Sankhya Darshan which is "Gyan Yoga" or knowledge, there are two words, "Purusha" (source of all consciousness), and "Prakriti" (matter}. Purusha is a formless God and Prakriti is perceived as manifestation of God in life form. God manifests in life which can be perceived through the senses. Purusha cannot be seen through the senses. Prakriti gives an opportunity to grow into Purusha or formless God. Those, who transcend Prakriti become Gods or Purusha, They sometime incarnate in human form on this planet to establish trust in God.

There are two major epics in India. One is "Mahabharata" the other is "Ramayana." Both these epics were written in Sanskrit language. Both these epics contain guidelines for spiritual growth through Nirgun and Sagun upasanas.

"Mahabharata" is the longest epic in the world. It is a narrative of Kurukhetra war which is the greatest war ever fought. It was a dynastic struggle for the throne of Hastinapur. There were two branches of a family; one is "Kauravas" the other is "Pandavas." The eldest amongst "Kauravas" was "Duryodhana." "Yudhishtir" was the eldest amongst "Pandavas." "Yudhishtir" was elder to "Duryodhana." Both claimed to be the inheritors of the throne.

The struggle culminates in the Great War in Kurukhetra. Pandavas ultimately become victorious.

Before the battle, Arjuna falls into despair because he finds it difficult to fight the war with his own cousins and relatives on the other side.

Krishna who is an incarnation of Vishnu reminds Arjuna of his duty as a "Kshatriya."

The section which describes the dialogue between Krishna and Arjuna is known as "Srimad Bhagvat Gita." It contains 18 chapters. Each chapter is termed "Yoga." Krishna tells in numerous ways to Arjuna how to transcend mind and become centered. Arjuna suffered from a wavering mind in the battlefield. Gita is a story of an indecisive man who wavers in mind and does not know what to do in conflicting situations.

Jagadguru Shankaracharya tells about personal and impersonal gods in the following verse:

"Mūrtaṁ chaivāmūrtaṁ dwe eva brahmaṇo rūpe,
ityupaniṣhat tayorvā dwau

Bhaktau bhagavadupadiṣhṭau, kleṣhādakleṣhādwā
muktisyāderatayormadhye"

"The Supreme entity is both personal and impersonal. Practitioners of the spiritual path are also of two kinds—devotees of the formless Brahman, and devotees of the personal form. But the path of worshipping the formless is very difficult."

The devotee of personal form (Bhakti Yoga) is the highest yogi.

Divine spirits, therefore, take human form (incarnate) on this planet for the growth of consciousness in human beings. The sin increases on this planet because of unconsciousness in man.

Both the Indian epics describe victory of the divine energy over evil energies. Rama fought Ravana who despite his wide knowledge and intellect was an egoist. Rama was a divine incarnation in human form and came to this planet when evil forces (intellect) became predominant. Similar is the mythology of Mahabharata and Krishna incarnating this planet.

Those who incarnate have full control over nature or Prakriti.

Neem Karoli Baba had control over Prakriti. Neem Karoli Baba did so many miracles only to prove that nature's laws can be transcended by divine incarnations. His miracles are described in the books written by his devotees both in India and in the west. Hanuman was also endowed with powers to transcend laws of nature. But we have not seen Hanuman in human form; therefore various mythologies around him appear to be unbelievable. But Neem Karoli Baba was seen by many in visible human form performing miracles that proves he could transcend nature's laws. Those miracles were performed to bring trust to us about divine incarnations.

Neem Karoli Baba is an incarnation in human form of Lord Hanuman. He came on this planet to revive the spirit of devotion and prayer through Rama and Hanuman. At this time, evil forces are predominant on this planet and unless divine energies descend there is no hope.

Earth is one of the few planets where life has evolved. In the solar system there is no life anywhere else. It is presumed that life might have existed on Mars but it has become extinct now because of abundance of Carbon di Oxide and depletion of Oxygen which is essential for sustenance of life.

Earth is also moving towards destruction because of deforestation and use of fossil fuel.

There is a possibility of life in at least 50,000 planets in the vast universe either in the primitive form or more advanced than on our planet.

The divine energies are spirits that support growth of consciousness on the planets where life exists.

Divine Energy

Before I discuss about divine energy, I shall like to say something about Energy.

For a long time it was thought that the universe is matter.

But thousands of years ago it was declared in India that matter is an illusion or "Maya."

It was not meant by these seers that matter does not exist. By illusion it was meant that it is not as it appears.

But now science has also come to accept that matter does not exist, it only appears to exist, and all matter is energy.

A new word "Quanta" has been coined. A "quanta" means particle and wave both at the same time.

Energy can only be waves, not particles.

Life is energy.

Energy can exist, it may also non-exist.

A star is the material form of energy that exists. A black hole is also an intense energy field created when the star dies.

We are born out of energy. The body is the material form of energy that can be seen. When the body dies, the visible energy becomes invisible that we call spirit.

Creation and destruction are two aspects of energy.

Whatever exists can also non-exist.

Whatever has birth has a death.

Everything in the universe has two dimensions; nothing is one-dimensional.

We can normally perceive only one side of the coin; the other side is hidden beneath and cannot be perceived.

Those who believe that existence is all and deny non-existence are seeing only one side of existence, the play of life.

To see only one side of the coin is ignorance. Ignorance means to know only one half.

To cling to one side is ignorance.

One who says I am born but I won't die is clinging to one half.

Pleasure and pain are not separate.

Light and darkness are not separate.

They are relative terms. Light is less darkness, Darkness is less light.

This duality of energy is best expressed by the Chinese symbol of "Yin" and "Yang."

It is futile to choose from the dual nature of energy. Meditation means choice less awareness.

If happiness comes, misery is hidden behind. If misery comes, happiness is hidden behind. They are part of the same coin.

Consciousness and unconsciousness are also two aspects of existence.

Both exist but one is conscious and the other is unconscious.

We eat food which is unconscious. But the energy that we receive from food makes us conscious.

The seers of the Upanishads said "Annam Brahma," meaning food is God.

All the religions in India accept reincarnation. After death or before birth we remain in the spirit form and are born again and again, life after life until all our desires are fulfilled and we are free. That is the ultimate freedom or Moksha.

Those who are liberated have a choice to be born and incarnate. They visit this planet in human form from time to time for deliverance of those who are seeking and searching.

Ram, Hanuman, Neem Karoli Baba are divine energies incarnated in human form for protection of good from evil.

It is said that when Buddha died 25 centuries ago he had predicted to take one more birth after 25 centuries in the form of Maitreya. There was a movement of Theosophical Society to bring Buddha to a human body since no womb was available for his birth. A number of spirits were sending messages which are recorded in the books of Theosophical society. But the movement of Theosophical Society failed because J. Krishnamurti denied. Krishnamurti became enlightened and became independent of any organization.

As already mentioned, in India there are two ways to grow consciousness.

One is the path of will and the other is the path of surrender.

Will does not require a God. Buddhism and Jainism which were born in India denied existence of God. Their path was the path of will and not of surrender or devotion.

Patanjali the great seer compiled "Yoga Sutras." This is known as "Raja Yoga."

The definition of Yoga given by Patanjali is as follows:

"योग: चित्त-वृत्ति निरोध:

yogah citta-vrtti-nirodhah"

— ***Yoga Sutras 1.2***

Yoga is the cessation of mind.

This definition is perhaps the best definition of Yoga.

When there is total hopelessness, utter despair one can understand the mind and its disturbances.

Cessation of these disturbances is Yoga.

Yoga is concerned with the mind.

Mind means a dreaming mind, which hopes.

Yoga means to come out of the dreaming mind.

Hopelessness means that there is no more hope.

One can enter Yoga only when one is totally frustrated with no hopes anymore.

At this point one becomes interested to know what is.

Hope only prolongs misery.

Baba used to say, "Those who are in sorrow are closer to God."

This is known "Dukkha" by Buddha.

Yoga is pure science. It is not Hindu, not Muslim, and not Christian.

After all everyone has mind and worries.

Yoga says don't believe and don't disbelieve.

Yoga is experiential, experimental.

Baba would say don't trust, don't distrust, even if you have to recite Sita – Ram, Sita – Ram mechanically, recite it and experiment.

That is Bhakti Yoga.

When an utter hopelessness arises, one is closer to God. No philosophy or rationalizations help. Baba said "Surrender to a divine even mechanically in the beginning and soon a trust would arise and you shall be free from anxieties."

Neem Karoli Baba has opened a door for surrender. He says, "Why worry unnecessarily; when I am there (to handle your worries).

For the modern age man, devotion and prayer is the true path. "Sagun Upasana" is the only path. Neem Karoli Baba has made it clear to the present age man that no other path but recitation of "Sita-Ram Sita – Ram" "Sunderkand" and "Hanuman Chalisa" is the only path to grow consciousness on this planet.

That is how this planet can be saved.

Baba has emphasized trust in a divine form of God. He emphasized Rama and Lord Hanuman to be the saviors of man in Kali Yuga.

3
Lord Hanuman and Neem Karoli Baba

I would like to differentiate between religion and spirituality.

As already discussed, the purpose of spirituality is to take man out of misery. Misery is a human phenomenon.

All the religions in the world were born through some master or prophet who realized divine experiences. Divine experiences take a man beyond mind to a state of bliss or non-misery.

Those who attained to divine experience radiated a different kind of vibration or energy, which seemed to come from some other world.

Those who came in contact with some realized soul felt the first – hand divine experience being near them.

With the passage of time, these experiences were passed on to the next generations through some scripture or word of mouth or memory.

In India, before scriptures were written, the messages and experiences of masters were transmitted through memory. When this was memorized, it was called "Smriti." If it was heard, it was called "Shruti."

Through "Shruti" or "Smiriti" or recorded scriptures, the words of the masters could be passed on to the posterity. But words fail to pass on the divine experiences.

Therefore with the passage of time, a tradition or cult is formed which becomes a religion around these masters. Holy Bible, Holy Quran, Bhagvat Gita and many other scriptures are the revelations that were recorded by those who heard it. Jesus Christ, Mohammed, Krishna and others are realized masters.

With the passage of time, mediatory agents called priests also came into being. They were interpreters of these scriptures. They also engaged in various religious practices. Priesthood thus became a profession around various religions. Temples, Churches, Mosques were also established as sacred places for worship by different religions.

With the advancement of science, it has now become possible to record in audio/video format words of the enlightened masters. Thus the audio/video recorded discourses of the modern age masters like Osho, J Krishnamurti etc are available. The need for intermediaries, priests and interpreters is now over. The words of the masters can directly be acquired by a seeker through these recordings.

Spirituality is different from religion. It is a direct experience by those who are close to a master.

There are many enlightened persons on this planet who realized divine experiences. But all the enlightened persons could not become a master. A master is one who is also capable of leading a seeker towards spirituality. Therefore, an enlightened person may not necessarily be a master. One can simply sit near him and feel divine experience and love.

In India, the word "Upanishad" literally means sitting close to a master.

Neem Karoli Baba also transmitted divine energy to those who were near him. They experienced his love. There are no recorded lectures or books by Baba. But the divine energy was felt by the devotees of Baba. The devotees recorded their experiences in various books. That is the only source available to understand and feel Baba even by those who never met or saw him.

As mentioned in the previous chapter, India has been a land of many spiritual paths. It has been an open society, not dogmatic. Hinduism accepted and absorbed everyone who has a message for the seeker.

With so many paths, it becomes difficult for a seeker to choose a path in the absence of a true master.

Karma Yoga, Gyan Yoga, Bhakti Yoga and Raja Yoga are different paths described by various masters in Hinduism. The ancient "Sutras" of Patanjali, Krishna, and Shiva etc are available in Sanskrit which facilitates understanding of the meaning of different spiritual paths.

Body, mind, heart and soul are four layers of human existence. Soul is the centre. Body, mind and heart are circles around the soul. Body is the farthest circle.

Karma Yoga belongs to the body in action.

Gyan Yoga belongs to the intellect or the mind. Mind is closer to the centre than the body. Gyan Yoga is closer to the centre than Karma Yoga. Karma Yoga pertains to the outermost periphery.

Bhakti Yoga belongs to the heart, it is closest to the centre. Through Bhakti it is easier to reach to the centre.

And finally Raja Yoga where nothing is required, it is the path of Sufis and Zen or meditation.

I would like to briefly describe these for a western seeker.

Karma Yoga

Karma Yoga is the way of action. Karma Yoga is an act with total absorption to offer your action to God. Karma Yoga is being in action without being the doer. You let God do. You efface yourself. If somebody is ill, go and serve and give him medicine. This is a selfless service. Something has to be done.

Neem Karoli Baba and Hanuman are both action – oriented. If someone cries for help and is in trouble, they have to do something. They do it on behalf of Rama, the Lord. That is why Hanuman is called "Sankat Mochan."

I would like to mention about a devotee of Neem Karoli Baba, whom Baba entrusted to be in "Karma Yoga."

Larry Brilliant who was a hippie doctor in America stumbled upon Neem Karoli Baba in the 1970's and became a devotee. Baba asked him to go into Karma Yoga. He prophesied that his role was to eradicate small pox, a deadly disease from the world. Larry wanted to be close to Baba to meditate, but Baba kept on insisting him to go to WHO office in Delhi to work for small pox.

Larry has written the entire account in his book "Sometimes brilliant." This book is a spiritual thriller. It is an interesting story how Brilliant worked hard and finally became successful in eradication of small pox from the globe. In those days, both USA and Soviet Russia were in cold war with each other but agreed to participate jointly in this mission for eradication of small pox.

This is an example of Karma Yoga. Subsequently, Larry established another organization, "Seva Foundation" for curing blindness and eye related diseases, which are working in several countries around the world.

This is an example of selfless service. Larry Brilliant worked like a true devotee of Baba. Larry worked selflessly like Hanuman, a devotee of Lord Rama.

There are many examples in the books written by Baba's devotees where incidences are described how Baba helped troubled souls to overcome worries. People call it Baba's miracles. Miracles happen and Baba is an example of such selfless service in the modern age. Hanuman is a living deity on this planet; He is helping the troubled souls. Baba and Hanuman mean one and the same thing.

The goal of Karma Yoga is freedom or "Moksha."

Gyan Yoga

Gyan Yoga is the pure path of knowing. There is nothing to be done. One has to drop the prejudices and concepts which can interfere with the truth. Whatever it is, one has to just see it. And that changes the person. To know the truth is to be transformed. The goal of the Gyan Yoga or the path of knowledge is to know truth.

Vedanta, Hinduism, Sankhya, Ashtavakra, J. Krishnamurti are on the path of Gyan Yoga. "Thou art that," says the Upanishad. Once you know that you become that.

Neem Karoli Baba did not preach any philosophy, did not deliver discourses, there are no books published by him. Though he was a Mahayogi, an incarnation, he did not ask his devotees to go into Gyan Yoga. He laid more emphasis in Karma and Bhakti Yoga. Hanuman is a total yogi; His life is more in the service of the Lord i.e. in Karma Yoga. He is a devotee of Lord Rama i.e. a "Bhakta." Baba is an incarnation of Hanuman.

Bhakti Yoga

Bhakti Yoga is the path of feeling. Love is the goal.

The path of Bhakti is whole; both Karma Yoga and Gyan Yoga are partial.

Vaishanavism, Christianity, Islam and others belong to the path of Bhakti or prayer.

The devotee changes the deity or God and vice versa. Both interact mutually.

Rama and Hanuman are interdependent. One who remembers and prays to Rama automatically becomes a devotee of Hanuman. Both merge into each other. Rama and Sita live in the heart of Hanuman.

Raja Yoga

This is the royal path or Raja Yoga.

With the previous three paths something remains in the mind, but in Raja Yoga no effort is there. You simply accept whatsoever is there. This acceptance is transcendence. You remain just a witness. There is no goal. You simply relax in your being.

With Karma Yoga there is a goal, the goal of freedom. With Gyan Yoga the goal is to know the truth. With Bhakti Yoga the goal is love. With Raja Yoga there is no goal. Zen and Sufism belong to Raja Yoga. As Basho has said,

"Sitting quietly, doing nothing, spring comes,

And the grass grows, by itself."

Raja Yoga is the path of meditation.

India has accepted all the spiritual practices. But it is like a dense forest where one is bound to get lost.

One must be able to choose a path that is suitable for one's individuality.

In Hinduism, God is defined as having three attributes. These are: Sat, Chit, Anand meaning Truth, Consciousness and Bliss.

Sat or Truth

As already explained, there is a difference between truth and reality. Reality is that which is perceptible to human senses. Truth is that which is beyond the sensory perceptions. The goal of all spiritual practices in Hinduism is to realize truth.

Chit or Consciousness

Another attribute of God is consciousness.

As already explained earlier, life evolves into consciousness. Man is partially conscious. The major part still remains unconscious. God is fully conscious. Therefore another goal of spirituality in Hinduism is to evolve consciousness. One who is fully conscious is called an enlightened person. Enlightened persons have a God – like quality. Buddha, Mahavira, Jesus, Mohammed and other enlightened masters are fully evolved in consciousness.

Anand or Bliss

Buddha has defined bliss as absence of sorrow.

Man lives in misery and happiness. Misery and happiness alternate. But bliss is beyond all miseries and happiness. It is a state of transcendence.

The aim of all spirituality in Hinduism is to attain to a state of bliss.

I would like to mention here that Buddha spoke of four noble truths. According to Buddha life is misery. The four noble truths are:

- Suffering exists.
- Suffering arises from attachment to desires.
- Suffering ceases when attachment to desires ceases.
- Freedom from suffering is possible by practicing the Eightfold Path

The path of Buddha was not the path of devotion. Buddha denied a God in form. His path was the path of meditation. When suffering ceases, one reaches the state of bliss or "Anand."

Path of Devotion

Hanuman and Neem Karoli Baba provide a clear-cut guideline for the modern – age man through the path of devotion to attain to Sat, Chit and Anand. Lord Rama is God. Hanuman and Neem Karoli Baba provide protection to those in sorrow so as to lead a life without sorrow. Through this protection the sorrow or misery is taken care of and one can transcend to the state of bliss or "Anand." If one is closer to Rama, then one is shielded by Hanuman in times of misery.

Lord Rama has given instruction to Hanuman to remain on the earth until the end of Kaliyug to protect from mundane problems those who are Lord's devotees. Mother Sita has blessed Hanuman for immortality. That is the reason Hanuman is called "Sankat Mochan" which means one who redeems from anxiety and worries.

Hanuman and Neem Karoli Baba are on the path of devotion and prayer in Kaliyug.

Tulsidas wrote in Ram Charit Manas:

"एहिं कलिकाल न साधन दूजा। जोग जग्य जप तप ब्रत पूजा।।
रामहि सुमिरिअ गाइअ रामहि। संतत सुनिअ राम गुन ग्रामहि।।

"Ehi Kali Kal Na Sadhan Duja,

Jog Jagya Jap Tap Vrat Puja

Ramahi Sumiriya Gaiya Ramahi,

Santat Suniya Ram Guna Gramahi"

Which means that "during the Kali Yug (Modern age) there is no other alternative, difficult spiritual practices (Sadhana) and rituals will not be of any help, one should only remember and chant the name of Rama. One should constantly listen to the attributes of the Lord."

Neem Karoli Baba said, "No Sadhana or spiritual practice is needed, and you shall become mad." Simply recite "Sita – Ram, Sita – Ram," Hanuman Chalisa and Sunderkand

He did not even insist on devotion or trust as a prerequisite to prayer. "Even if you recite mechanically, you shall one day stumble upon the true Rama," he said.

> "रामहि सुमिरिअ गाइअ रामहि। संतत सुनिअ राम गुन ग्रामहि।।"
>
> *"Ramahi Sumiriya Gayia Ramahi, Santat Suniya Ram Gun Gramahi"*
>
> *Meaning thereby "Remember Rama, recite Rama, constantly remember the attributes of Rama"*

Neem Karoli Baba who himself is an incarnation of Hanuman made it simple to choose a Devata out of the crores of devis and devatas in Indian mythology. He chose only Hanuman. Why?

The answer is given by Goswami Tulsidas who wrote in Hanuman Chalisa:

> *"Aur devatā chitta Na dharaī |*
> *hanumata sei sarva sukha karaī"*
>
> **MEANING:** *"One need not contemplate on any other deity; by serving Hanuman one can attain to all happiness and bliss"*

There is a story of Hanuman in Ramayana.

According to Valmiki's Ramayana, one morning in his childhood, Hanuman was hungry and saw the rising red colored Sun. Mistaking it for a ripe fruit, he leapt up to eat it.

Tulsidas in Hanuman Chalisa writes:

> *"Yug Sahastra Yojana par bhanu, Lilyo tahi madhur phal (Delicious fruit) janu"*
>
> **MEANING :** *The Surya, sun situated 96,000,000 miles or 153,600,000 km from the earth, was swallowed by you assuming it to be a sweet fruit.*

The king of gods, Indra intervened and struck his thunderbolt.

It hit Hanuman on his jaw, and he fell to the earth unconscious with a broken jaw. His father, Vayu (air), became upset and withdrew.

The lack of air created immense suffering to all living beings on earth.

This led Brahma, the god of life, to intervene and resuscitate Hanuman, which in turn prompted Vayu to return to the living beings.

Thus life on planet earth revived.

All the gods and goddesses bestowed their divine energy to Hanuman. Thus Hanuman is the only god who is bestowed with divine energy of all the gods and goddesses. Therefore, if one worships only Hanuman he receives the divine energy of all the gods and goddesses.

Even if one serves Hanuman and no other Devata, they obtain all worldly and other-worldly bliss. This is because only Hanuman is endowed with divine energy of all gods and goddesses.

Anxiety, Anguish, Despair, Hopelessness, Meaninglessness, "Sankat_

Today the human beings on this planet are living life in anxiety, anguish, fear, despair, hopelessness and meaninglessness. This is called "Sankat." So we need to invoke "Sankat Mochan" or Hanuman to overcome this hopelessness. Neem Karoli Baba is an incarnation of Hanuman.

Life on this planet in the last about 200 years has seen a decline of trust in God. The development of science and technology changed the earlier society from an agricultural to be an industrial society.

This has changed the outlook of the planet completely.

The planet has witnessed two World Wars which caused untold destruction and killed millions. Destructive energies have grown beyond limits. These are "Asuri" energies, which are now dominating the planet.

Hitler, Mussolini, Stalin, Mao etc are human forms of destructive energies.

Both the World Wars were fought in Europe.

No war was fought in America. America supplied war weapons, arms and ammunitions to all the warring European countries; it became rich and accumulated great wealth.

America is today the richest country in the world. It still thrives on sale of war material.

America can easily be compared to the Lanka in the times of Lord Rama.

Lanka was ruled by Ravana, it was a country full of gold. Destructive energies thrived. Rama had to be incarnated in human form to destroy destructive energy and re-establish a civilization where one could lead a life of bliss.

Like Lanka of Treta Yuga, America is a land of gold (now converted into Dollars). Because of immense strength, wealth and power America is a terror to the entire world in this age of Kaliyuga.

The world is now fighting a different kind of war. The world has become intelligent in Kaliyug. Now war is not to be fought in the battle – field.

Through control of economy, an economic war is killing millions. Every nation in the world is under huge debts through World Bank loans in the name of development. Each country is forced to repay these loans through taxation, causing sufferings, poverty, and hunger to millions everywhere.

After the devastation of Europe in the two world wars, the European countries decided not to fight amongst themselves. They created a union known as European Union to create a common market and a common currency. But they have still not been able to emerge out of the economic crisis despite all treaties and agreements.

After the Second World War, a new strategy for sale of war material has emerged known as "terrorism."

World Bank was created after the Second World War. World Bank is a strategy to keep the nations dependent for loans and borrowings.

World Bank through the network of Banks around the world can be compared to the money changers in the times of Jesus. The merchants and money changers in the temples of Jerusalem were driven away by Jesus because temples of prayers had become a house of trade. Those very Jewish merchants are now creating economic havoc in the world today through World Bank, Stock markets, trade, commerce and money lending. Religious organisations are working hands – in – glove with these merchants.

In the Islamic world interest on loans is forbidden by Islam.

But contrary to these religious beliefs, the world is dominated by loans and interests.

With the development of Science in the west, trust in God has received a big jolt.

Friedrich Nietzsche, the German philosopher was able to foresee the shape of things to come. He proclaimed very early that "God is dead." The reason was that he realized that the so – called "Abrahimic God" was killed by science. With the development of science the very purpose of life was lost. God had served the basis and purpose for meaning and value in the west for thousands of years. Science killed God. Doubt reigned supreme and trust was lost. Science was based on doubt, spirituality was based on trust.

Subsequently, in the west, existentialists like Soren Kierkegaard, Heidegger, Sartre, Camus, Kafka and many others philosophized that the world was meaningless, full of negativity, anxiety, anguish and dread.

Jean-Paul Sartre declared that "Man is condemned to be free."

The Second World War and the events that followed thereafter set a framework of a world of fear, despair and hopelessness.

Science gave rise to materialism. Science took away man's trust in a divine source.

Communism was born because it believed matter to be the only truth. It denied religion totally. Stalin killed millions who were suspected to be part of some religious belief. China where Confucianism, Taoism and Buddhism had thrived for thousands of years became atheist after it became communist.

After the downfall of communism in Soviet Russia in 1992, priesthood and religions have again entered the communist countries.

When China attacked India in 1962, someone asked Baba about this invasion. Baba said that communism cannot enter India. The roots of religion are so deep in India that it cannot become a communist country, Baba clarified.

He was then asked the reason for this Chinese attack on India. Baba said that the Chinese attack was primarily intended to awaken India.

Shortly afterwards, the Chinese returned.

The consequence of scientific development and communism has been a major cause of hopelessness and meaninglessness to human beings on this planet.

The world of Science and materialism has been the major cause of hopelessness on this planet.

This is 'Sankat.' It is necessary to revive God in the west to come out of their despondency.

But instead of traditional priesthood and religions, what the west needs today is a universal God. This universal God is Rama and Hanuman. Rama is God and Hanuman a living deity and devotee of Rama known as "Sankat Mochan."

The existentialists in the west did not know the way out of the hopelessness. Their trust in God received a jolt. For the existentialist philosophers suicide was the only way out.

The west did not know about the word "Sankat."

They – also did not know anything about Hanuman, a "Sankat Mochan," one who can redeem from hopelessness.

What is "Sankat"?

Sankat means insecurity, danger, distress, difficulty, despair, worry, anxiety, hopelessness etc.

There are situations in life when one moves between hope and frustration. Even in situations where one is frustrated, there is still some hope that things may change. This is not "Sankat" or hopelessness.

But sometimes, life takes such a turn that one reaches the dead end and there is no hope. This is different from frustration. It is utter hopelessness. This hopelessness is "Sankat."

George Gurdjieff called it "dark night of the soul."

Existentialists call it "Angst" or "Dread" or "Meaninglessness."

For the existentialist, in such utter hopelessness, suicide is the only answer.

But contrary to the western existentialists, Neem Karoli Baba said "I love sorrow. It brings me closer to God."

Only in such a hopeless situation, it is possible to come closer to God. This is contrary to the belief of the western existentialist.

In a hopeless situation, either there is an option to commit suicide or to develop trust in God or existence.

The west has chosen the option of suicide. The East has chosen the option of a divine support.

In such hopelessness, Hanuman and Neem Karoli Baba are the saviors.

Today the west needs Hanuman and Neem Karoli Baba more than anything else to overcome anxiety and despair.

One has to surrender to the divine.

That is why Neem Karoli Baba said that in such moment's one is closer to God.

In moments of utter hopelessness, mind is unable to logically analyze and rationalize the cause and how to come out of such a situation.

Tulsidas in Hanuman Chalisa also says:

>"साधु सन्त के तुम रखवारे ।
>असुर निकन्दन राम दुलारे ॥३०॥"

"Sadhu Sant Ke Tum Rakhvare, Asur Nikandan Ram Dulare"

"You are the protector of saints and sages. You destroy the Demons; you are dear to Shri Ram"

Sadhu and Asur

What is the meaning of "Sadhu" and "Asur"?

There is a lot of confusion about the word "Sadhu" in India.

Often by "Sadhu" one understands a monk, who is engaged in various kinds of spiritual practices. That is not the correct meaning.

Merely by becoming a renunciate or a monk, or an ascetic, one does not become a Sadhu. There are about 4 to 5 million Sadhus in India. They belong to Vaishnav or Shaiva or in some cases Shakta traditions. There are many subgroups.

For Hanuman a "Sadhu" is one who is pure in heart, sensitive, empathetic, who does not hurt anyone, is compassionate.

In this world there are very few who can be called "Sadhus."

Because the society teaches struggle for survival, it makes one cunning and selfish. Competition and ambition make a man "Asur."

A cunning person is "Asur." A Sadhu often becomes gullible to a person with "Asuri" nature.

In terms of modern psychology, a "Sadhu" is one with higher consciousness. An "Asur" is one who is living in unconsciousness.

Hanuman protects the "Sadhus" from "Asur." He is a protector to those who are pure in heart, simple in nature and who are surrounded by evil energies.

In short, Hanuman helps in raising the consciousness in man.

Hanuman and Neem Karoli Baba – A Universal Deity

Hanuman is one deity where no cult exists around him. There are cults around Vishnu and Shiva known as "Vaishnavism" and "Shaivism." "Shaktism" is also a tradition in Hinduism where feminine or "Devi" goddess is supreme.

As already discussed, in Kaliyug, "Asurs" or evil forces dominate the earth much more compared to the previous ages.

Man is torturing man, there is inequality in society, poor countries suffer from poverty, and survival is becoming difficult.

Therefore, there is an urgent need to promote divine energies to protect man to live in peace. This can be done only by seeking the support of Hanuman who is a devotee and sets an example of true service to Lord Rama.

There is no "ism" around Hanuman. An "ism" is a belief system. No one goes to worship Hanuman because one belongs to a particular faith. People worship "Vishnu" or "Shiva" or Goddess "Durga," or "Kali" because of established cults.

Hanuman represents a God in form whose worship takes one out of troubles. He is called "Sankat Mochan" which means one who can take away all the troubles.

Neem Karoli Baba also did not establish a cult around him. People belonging to different cultures, faith and cult came to him and received his divine energy. He was an ardent devotee of Lord Rama and Hanuman.

It is a miracle that Baba did not preach; there are no recorded lectures, no books written by Baba. No scripture can therefore be created around Baba. Without a scripture no cult or organization can be created.

Around all the masters of the world scriptures were created by their followers. Therefore organized religions were formed, be it Jesus, Moses or Muhammad, Buddha, Mahavira or any other religion.

Once a religion is established it loses the spirit of prayer, devotion, and meditation.

But because no scriptures can be created around Neem Karoli Baba it cannot become a religion. It would be spread only through individual experience of the devotees.

Those who came to Baba during his lifetime were pulled by his magnetic force and were instantly transformed to become a devotee. Even when he is not in physical form now, his presence is felt strongly by many who are pulled by his divine energy. It can be felt and experienced but cannot be described. I never saw or met him, but to me his pull is felt strongly. That is the reason of my writing this book.

The conscious mind functions only in logic and rationality. When it finds that logic is of no help in a hopeless situation, it drops. Only in such moments of utter frustration, one can transcend and come nearer to truth.

In such a hopeless situation, Hanuman comes to one's rescue.

Neem Karoli Baba helped many in such hopeless situations.

He was also "Sankat Mochan."

Both Hanuman and Neem Karoli Baba exist and should not be termed as "Was," instead they "Are."

Both are immortal. They exist now in the spirit form to help those who are in "Sankat."

Rama is the source of Hanuman's divine energy. Without Rama one cannot worship Hanuman.

Since these divine souls have not been experienced in human form by us, they incarnate to remind us of their divine power.

Neem Karoli Baba is an incarnation of Hanuman in human form. Baba said that those who are in sorrow are closer to God. His primary concern was to make one trouble – free. This he did with his divine powers which people call "Miracles."

Neem Karoli Baba came to this planet to awaken the spirit of prayer through Hanuman. He had spiritual powers through "Siddhi's" or spiritual practices. Through his "Siddhi's" he only tried to prove that divine powers in Hanuman is not a matter of fiction, it exists to support the humans from obstacles to spiritual growth. Neem Karoli Baba is one of the mysterious happenings on this planet which is unbelievable.

What are Siddhi's?

In Hanuman Chalisa Tulsidas writes:

"अष्ट सिद्धि नव निधि के दाता, अस बर दीन जानकी माता."

"By the grace of mother Sita, Hanuman grants to his devotees divine powers through Siddhi's."

These Siddhi's are:

Anima: reducing one's body even to the size of an atom

Mahima: expanding one's body to an infinitely large size

Garima: becoming infinitely heavy

Laghima: becoming almost weightless

Prāpti: ability to be anywhere at will

Prākāmya: realizing whatever one desires

Iṣtva: supremacy over nature

Vaśtva: control of natural forces

Lord Hanuman had all the above Siddhi's; he could make his body large and small through Siddhi's.

In Hanuman Chalisa, Tulsidas writes:

> **"Sukshma Roop Dhari Siyahi Dikhava**
> **Vikat Roop Dhari Lank Jarava"**
>
> **"You appeared before Sita in a Diminutive form and spoke to**
> **Her in humility**
> **You assumed an awesome form and struck**
> **Terror by setting Lanka on fire"**

Neem Karoli Baba was also gifted with all the Siddhi's. It has been reported by his devotees that he could become heavy, lightweight, could be anywhere at will, convert water into milk, Ghee or petrol. These miraculous powers are acquired through Siddhi's. He did all these miracles through "Siddhi's" to help the troubled ones or those in "Sankat."

Jesus was also endowed with such Siddhi's. He was also able to bring life to the dead, eyes to the blind.

Nature was under the control of Neem Karoli Baba.

Devotion and prayer are very personal and individual.

Neem Karoli Baba did not preach trust as a precondition to prayer. He would ask to recite "Sita – Ram, Sita – Ram" even mechanically and said one day it would become trust.

In Gita, Krishna talks about prayer as follows:

श्रेयो हि ज्ञानमभ्यासाज्ज्ञानाद्ध्यानं विशिष्यते |
ध्यानात्कर्मफलत्यागस्त्यागाच्छान्तिरनन्तरम् ||12||

Shreyo hi jñānam abhyāsāj jñānād dhyānaṁ viśhiṣhyate

Dhyānāt karma-phala-tyāgas tyāgāch chhāntir anantaram

"Better than mechanical practice is knowledge; better than knowledge is meditation, better than meditation is renunciation of the fruits of actions, for peace immediately follows such renunciation"

Baba said the same thing to his devotees what Krishna has said in the above verse.

Someone asked Baba "If we cannot pray with devotion then it would be nothing but hypocrisy."

Baba replied "You cannot pray with devotion and you can also not pray mechanically without devotion, what you want to do then?"

He said in the beginning everyone prays mechanically without devotion. But as heart starts becoming pure then true prayer and devotion begin. He was therefore in favor of even praying mechanically. He said God is not something to be seen through our physical eyes. One needs to develop an insight, which is only possible through the purity of heart. "Recite name of Rama even mechanically, one day true Ram would happen and one can be free" Baba would say.

His message was simple. Recite "Sita – Ram Sita – Ram," "Hanuman Chalisa" or "Sunder Kand" and all your worries would be taken care of by Hanuman.

Chanting and Prayer

How does recitation help?

If we understand in terms of modern psychology, constant practice of chanting goes deeper into our subconscious or unconscious mind.

This is how we learn. If we have to learn driving, at first it is a conscious effort. Once we learn, it goes deeper in our consciousness and becomes an automatic activity. You don't have to remember it consciously. This learning goes into our unconsciousness.

In a similar way continuous chanting of "Sita – Ram Sita – Ram" would one day become part of our unconscious mind and with devotion it would take away our miseries caused by the thinking mind.

Do not doubt, do not even trust but experiment through chanting and recitation of Hanuman and Ram. It is like a scientific experimentation. Have patience, do not worry and do not hurry. One day suddenly the trust would arise.

One would even start having visions in dreams and religious experiences in the subconscious mind.

Those who went to Neem Karoli Baba were attracted by his subtle energy. He was capable of easily taking a person into "Samadhi" which is the transcendental state and divine. In the books written by his devotees, such experiences are described in detail and one can read about them.

Therefore the purpose of prayer is to elevate our energy level to exalted states, which can easily happen when one is around an enlightened master. That is the reason why a "Sat Guru "or a master was needed for further growth.

Neem Karoli Baba is an incarnation. His divine energy is still felt by devotees even by those who never came in contact with him while he was alive.

Enlightened Persons, Masters and Incarnations

India has been a country where many masters have existed from time to time. Hindus believe that without a master spiritual growth is not possible.

One should clearly understand the difference between a non-believer, follower, disciple and a devotee.

A non-believer has no belief, no faith. A follower has a belief. A disciple trusts a master. A devotee is merged in God. He has experienced the divine.

A Master or a Guru having divine energy is capable of taking one to spiritual growth to realize God.

There have been many enlightened persons on this planet, who have realized full consciousness, but very few masters. All enlightened persons do not have the capability to be a master.

Many enlightened persons remain in hiding because it is difficult to express in that exalted state. They are introverts and cannot share their joy with others.

Masters are compassionate; they cannot live without sharing their joy.

Buddha is a master, Mahavira is a master, Krishna is a master, Patanjali is a master, Jesus is a master, Osho is a master but Neem Karoli Baba is a divine incarnation of lord Hanuman.

God is the highest level of divine energy.

Master is a medium that receives energy from God.

Disciple is one who is capable of receiving divine energy from a Master.

Everyone does not have that capability.

Masters pull disciples who are capable to receive the energy.

For the master, space and time are not barriers.

Hindus have worshipped masters more than God.

Hindus say

> *"Guru Gobind Dou Khade Kake Lagoon Pai,*
> *Balihari Guru Aapno, Govind Diyo Batay"*

Meaning thereby, if a Master and God are standing together and I have to choose whom to bow down I shall bow down to the master because he is the one who made me realize the God.

Hindus have a special day to worship a master each year. This is called "Guru Purnima." Purnima means full moon.

The Guru Purnima is celebrated in India each year in the month of "Ashadh" (June/July) on a full moon day.

Hindus have symbolized God with Sun. Sun has intense energy that cannot be directly seen. In the same way, the energy of God cannot be experienced and absorbed directly.

Master has been symbolized with Moon. Moon does not have its own energy. It derives its energy from Sun. But the energy of moon is cool and silent. In the same way, Master derives its energy from God, makes it cool and silent, which can be felt and experienced by the disciple. It is ecstatic.

Dark clouds hovering around moon in the rainy season (Ashadh month) are symbols of disciples. Disciples hover around the master with all their darkness in the same way as dark clouds hover around moon during rains. Through these dark clouds moon shines once in a while symbolizing the disciples whose darkness has been dispelled and cleared.

That is the mystery of a master.

Neem Karoli Baba is an incarnation. He is capable of raising the consciousness through his divine energy. He shows the path to meet the divine through gods like Hanuman and Rama.

Therefore we bow to the feet of Neem Karoli Baba, without whom we shall not be able to experience Hanuman and Rama.

A master is one who shows the path to disciples.

But Neem Karoli Baba never made disciples.

Those who came to him became devotees.

Devotee means a "Bhakta" of "Bhagwan" or God.

Bhagwan is one who listens to our prayers. He is interested in our mundane problems and through his compassion solves it. Neem Karoli Baba listened to our mundane problems. He did not give discourses.

Therefore, Neem Karoli Baba is not a master who makes disciples. He is an incarnation. There are very few incarnations on this planet. Rama is an incarnation, Krishna is an incarnation. Hanuman is an incarnation. Neem Karoli Baba is an incarnation. Incarnations do not make disciples. They make devotees or "Bhakta." There are devotees of Rama, Krishna, Hanuman and Neem Karoli Baba. Meera was a devotee of Krishna. Arjuna was not a devotee. He was only a friend of Krishna. That is the reason why he could not understand what Krishna told him in the eighteen chapters of Gita. Meera had never read Gita but became a devotee.

Hanuman and Rama are divine energies, to see them only in form and worship would not be of any help unless we can also feel their vibrations. These vibrations don't die, they are immortal. We have only to become a receiver of that divine energy. This is easily possible when a living master is around. Neem Karoli Baba is not only a living master but an incarnation.

How to choose a master? A true master cannot be chosen by a man.

A true master appears when the disciple is ready.

Let us now discuss about god Hanuman and his divine energy. Why should one worship Hanuman when there are so many deities?

In India, before the arrival of Aryans, there existed a Dravidian culture.

Hanuman is a fusion deity between Aryan and Pre-Aryan culture. As already mentioned earlier, India has not maintained historical records but various "Puranas" describe mythologies. Hanuman is mentioned both in Ramayana and Mahabharata epics which are the most ancient epics in India in Sanskrit language. Hanuman is mentioned in many Puranas and also in Buddhist, Jain and Sikh religious texts.

He is considered an incarnation of Lord Shiva, one of the three Hindu trinity gods. He is the devotee of Rama who is incarnation of Hindu god Vishnu. Thus Hanuman is a link between Shiva and Vishnu two prominent Hindu gods.

Hanuman-a fusion deity between Shiva and Vishnu

Further, Tulsidas writes about Hanuman:

"Charon yug partap tumhara, hai parsiddha jagat ujiyara"

MEANING – *"Your glory is famous in all the four Yugas* **(Satya, Treta, Dwapar and Kaliyug),** *and illuminates the whole world"*

"Yuga" in Hinduism is an epoch or era with four cycles.

The cycle starts with Satya Yuga and goes via Treta Yuga and Dvapara Yuga into Kali Yuga. Our present time is Kali Yuga. Kaliyuga started at 3102 BC, after the end of Kurukshetra or Mahabharat war, when Lord Krishna left the earth and went to His abode.

The ages see a gradual decline of dharma, wisdom, knowledge, intellectual capability, and life span as well as emotional and physical strength.

In Satya Yuga – Virtue reigns supreme. Human stature was 21 cubits. Average human lifespan was 100,000 years.

Treta Yuga – There was three – quarter virtue and one – quarter sin. Normal human stature was 14 cubits. Average human lifespan was 10,000 years.

Dwapara Yuga – There was one – half virtue & one – half sin. Normal human stature was 7 cubits. Average human lifespan was 1,000 years.

Kali Yuga – There is one – quarter virtue & three – quarter sin. Normal human stature is 3.5 cubits. Average human lifespan will be 100 years.

The above verse of Tulsidas refers to the Immortality and glory of Lord Hanuman in all the four Yugas or cyclic ages.

During Mahabharat war in Dwapara Yuga, Hanuman was sitting on the top of the flag of Arjun's chariort. The following verse in Gita is relevant:

"अथ व्यवस्थितान्दृष्ट्वा धार्तराष्ट्रान् कपिध्वजः ।

प्रवृत्ते शस्त्रसम्पाते धनुरुद्यम्य पाण्डवः ॥ 1/20॥

हृषीकेशं तदा वाक्यमिदमाह महीपते ।

Atha vyavasthitān dṛiṣhṭvā dhārtarāṣhṭrān kapi-dhwajaḥ

Pravṛitte śhastra-sampāte dhanurudyamya pāṇḍavaḥ

Hṛiṣhīkeśhaṁ tadā vākyam idam āha mahī-pate"

"At that time, the son of Pandu, Arjun, who had the insignia of Hanuman on the flag of his chariot, took up his bow. Seeing your sons arrayed against him, O King, Arjun then spoke the following words to Shree Krishna."

Hanuman is still a living deity on the earth in present times i.e. Kaliyug.

It is said that when Bhagwan Rama finished his divine play or "Leela" on this planet and was going to return to his heavenly abode, Hanuman prayed to him to go with him. But Lord Rama told Hanuman to stay back on earth till the end of "Kaliyug" to help those who were devotees of Rama to take them out of trouble. Hanuman is therefore a living deity on this earth and several devotees have reported visions of Hanuman even today. I spoke to a devotee of Baba who was a "pujari" in Neem Karori temple. He told me to have had visions of both Baba and Hanuman in the temple.

Neem Karoli Baba revived the spirit of Hanuman on the earth once again.

Both Hanuman and Neem Karoli Baba help the devotees through miracles.

Hanuman is a universal deity and does not belong only to India.

This book is intended to revive the spirit of Hanuman globally without distinction of nations, cultures, caste and creed.

Today Hanuman has become more relevant than in any other period because the planet is on the verge of extinction.

Devata is one who is empathetic.

Human beings only show sympathy.

Sympathy is only a lip service.

There is a vast difference between empathy and sympathy.

In empathy one feels the misery of others as if it is happening to him, and does everything possible to help the person to come out of the troubles.

Neem Karoli Baba is empathetic. He suffered others' miseries and helped to take them out of anxiety, worry and misery from mundane problems.

Hanuman is known as "Sankat Mochan." He is empathetic. Therefore, one who is passing through a difficult phase in life needs to be in touch with a divine energy like "Hanuman," who is empathetic. Miracle happens.

As already mentioned, Rama is a divine incarnation of Vishnu one of the trinity gods of Hindus.

The concept of incarnation is to be understood in terms of evolution of life on this planet.

It is understood that earth formed about 4.5 billion years ago. Within the first billion years life appeared in the oceans.

Fish or "Matsya" is the first Avatar (Incarnation) of Vishnu. Then as life evolved, Tortoise or "Kurma" avatar was born. Similarly, there are other Avatars totaling to ten, of which nine avatars have already happened and the tenth avatar as "Kalki" has yet to happen.

Rama is the seventh avatar and Krishna is the eight avatar of Vishnu.

The avatars are born when there is crisis on the planet. It happens when evil becomes stronger and the cosmos loses balance. The avatars are then born to destroy evil and to restore cosmic balance.

Rama and Krishna are most known and celebrated avatars in Hinduism. Mahabharat containing the Srimad Bhagvat Gita includes Krishna while Ramayana and Ram Charit Manas include Rama in several mythologies to describe their acts to remove evil forces from this planet.

Of these two Avatars Rama and Krishna, Rama is a householder devoted to his wife, parents, Guru, brothers etc and sets an example to the society for a harmonious living. Contrary to this Krishna breaks all the rules of the society but is considered by Hindus as a full incarnation or "Poorna Avatar." Krishna does not preach any morality.

We shall not go into the details but it would be sufficient to say that Rama sets devotion and prayer essential for growth of an individual, whereas Krishna is a Yogi. In Srimad Bhagvat Gita, which contains 18 chapters Krishna describes different Yogas for attainment or to come out of misery. It contains Gyan Yoga, Karma Yoga and Bhakti Yoga and various combinations but does not clearly describe which yoga one should choose. Rama, on the contrary only praises devotion and prayer as the true path and therefore it is easy to grasp by a devotee.

Therefore even though Krishna tried to explain to Arjuna various kinds of Yoga when he was in crisis and running away from the battlefield, yet Arjuna could not understand and thought it fit to fight the war.

In chapter 18 of Gita Krishna asks Arjuna whether he has understood what has been said to him:

The shloka 18.72 is as follows:

"कच्चिदेतच्छ्रुतं पार्थ त्वयैकाग्रेण चेतसा |
कच्चिदज्ञानसम्मोह: प्रनष्टस्ते धनञ्जय ||72||

Kachchid etach chhrutam pārtha tvayaikāgreṇa chetasā

kachchid ajñāna-sammohaḥ pranaṣhṭas Te dhanañjaya"

"O Arjun, have you heard me with a concentrated mind? Have your ignorance and delusion been destroyed?"

In shloka 73 of Chapter 18, Arjun says:

अर्जुन उवाच |
नष्टो मोह: स्मृतिर्लब्धा त्वत्प्रसादान्मयाच्युत |
स्थितोऽस्मि गतसन्देह: करिष्ये वचनं तव ||73|

Arjuna uvācha

naṣhṭo mohaḥ smṛitir labdhā tvat-prasādān mayāchyuta

sthito 'smi gata-sandehaḥ kariṣhye vachanam tava

"Arjun Said: O infallible one, by your grace my illusion has been dispelled, and I am situated in knowledge. I am now free from doubts, and I shall act according to your instructions."

Arjuna says "I shall act according to your instructions." Krishna had not given any instructions whether to fight the war or to escape. He only asked whether his illusions had been dispelled.

Arjuna was a warrior. He had gone to the battlefield to fight a war with his cousins. But he came under illusion and became indecisive whether to fight the war or to renounce since it was not a war with any outsider enemy but one with his own family members.

Arjuna had asked Krishna to dispel his doubts whether to fight the war or escape.

Krishna tried his best to explain in 18 chapters of Gita various methods to transcend doubts and to become decisive.

There are many situations in life when one becomes indecisive and does not know a clear-cut answer. In such situations one is bound to be worried. Gita is a story of such an indecisive man in doubt and in crisis.

Arjuna while answering Krishna whether his doubts had been dispelled said "I shall act according to your instructions."

In my view Arjuna thought it fit to fight the war instead of listening to further discourses from Krishna because Gita is confusing with such a wide variety of methods that it becomes difficult for one to choose.

We are also like Arjuna; we also get confused which path to choose when we are faced with a crisis. There are so many paths given to us that we get confused.

I was a disciple of "Osho." Osho is like Krishna. He has explained various paths through his discourses but ultimately leaves it to his disciples to choose what is fit for him. Osho was not accessible to discuss human mundane problems.

On the contrary, Neem Karoli Baba clearly explains that our path is that of devotion and prayer. Simply recite "Sita – Ram, Sita – Ram," Hanuman Chalisa and Sunder Kand and no other spiritual practice is required to overcome your worries.

Osho never spoke on Rama and Hanuman. He spoke extensively on Krishna and others. He did not clearly describe the path suitable for a disciple. He was not accessible to common masses for their mundane problems. Poverty was not an issue for him. He was therefore known as "Rich Man's Guru." He was more attuned to Krishna and did not lay down any rules for society. He was known as a Guru promoting "Free Sex." He was a controversial Guru and did not find acceptance with common masses. Osho's effort was to demolish all so – called religions and priesthood. He thought once old, rotten religions were destroyed, it was possible for man to begin with a clean slate without any preconceived faith or religious belief. He thought only after the old was demolished, a new structure could be created. He had envisioned a "New Man" who was totally free from all belief system, indoctrination. He called the "New Man" "Zorba the Buddha." This meant who lived in the world yet remained outside the world. This was a true spirituality. I can see his point but to what extent the new man would be materialized is yet to be seen. Before Osho left his body, he said to his disciples, "I leave you my dream."

I wonder about this statement. Osho had dreamt something. Firstly, dream is a dream, it is not a reality. Secondly, how the dream of someone could be fulfilled by others. This is a contradiction in terms. I think the dream of Osho would remain only a dream. I don't see any possibility of his dream being fulfilled by his disciples.

On the contrary, Neem Karoli Baba was accessible to common and poor people. He heard patiently and knew that unless mundane problems were solved, one cannot rise in spirituality. He never made disciples but those who came to him became devotees through his divine presence. He reestablished trust in Rama and Hanuman. His vision is to make Rama and Hanuman a universal God and deity beyond the boundaries of India. His vision seems to be fructified through his western devotees. Today a Hanuman Foundation in USA has been established and many people are becoming interested.

We need the support of divine incarnations who can remove our worries without difficult spiritual practices.

Hanuman is called "Sankat Mochan" because for him mundane human issues are more important than spiritual discourses. Neem Karoli Baba was also an incarnation of Hanuman and a "Sankat Mochan." Baba never gave any spiritual discourses. He used to say "I have not read much, I am uneducated."

For me Rama is more approachable and understandable than Krishna. For me Neem Karoli Baba is more approachable (even though I never met or saw him physically and have also not visited his temples and Ashrams) than "Osho."

Neem Karoli Baba used to say "Why worry when I am there." This puts more confidence in me than my Guru Osho who never said a word about mundane issues.

The story of Rama is our story. It is human. He was born a man, not a saint to preach. He was the eldest son of a King. He was eligible to sit on the throne after his father retired. But when his father decided to give the throne to Rama and retire, one of the three wives of Dashrath (Rama's father) intervened. She asked her husband Dashrath to fulfill two promises given earlier to her. He had to fulfill his promise to the queen whose name was "Kaikeyi." The queen wanted her son Bharat to be enthroned as a king instead of Rama, and wanted Rama to move to the forest and remain in exile for 14 years.

Kaikeyi was a tough woman?

But all woman are stronger than man, they are capable of emotional blackmail.

It is a human problem.

Dashrath had to yield to Kaikeyi.

The king died of sorrow and Rama had to go into exile with his wife Sita and younger brother Lakshman.

Thus the story begins.

The entire epic Ram Charit Manas shows respect and love amongst brothers, husband and wife. This respect and love in the family and society is vanishing causing untold misery. Baba always advocated love amongst the family members and gave special emphasis on the woman of the house to take care of the husband and children lovingly. The world today needs to read this epic and emulate the love. Unless love exists in the family and society, the planet is doomed.

Hanuman is one central character of the epic. Without Hanuman, the epic could not have been written. Hanuman is endowed with divine energy but is too human.

Rama, though an incarnation of Lord Vishnu goes through all the travails and agonies like a common man.

As the story goes, Parvati, the consort of Lord Shiva was very sad looking at the way Rama was living in exile with Sita and Lakshman.

She enquired from Lord Shiva the reason for difficult times Rama was passing through.

Shiva replied:

"Hoi hai soya Jo Ram rachi rakha, ko kari tarak barhavai sakha."

These lines are from Shri RamcharitraManas. Lord Shiva explains to Maa Parvati that everything happens according to the destiny. One should not have any argument, logic, analysis or rationalizations about what is destined.

Neem Karoli Baba and Hanuman both are "Sankat Mochan." They want to extricate us from difficult times.

Prayer and devotion also change destiny. Baba is capable of changing destiny.

Hanuman mitigated sufferings of Rama.

I would like to state that like Neem Karoli Baba, Jesus too was a human. He was empathetic to the poor and troubled. He also did miracles like Baba. He gave life to Lazarus. Finally, he suffered crucifixion because he was promising kingdom of God, which was understood by the king as an encroachment on his empire. It is said that Jesus had visited India before his crucifixion and was more in tune with eastern methods than the Jewish God who was very cruel and inhuman. The Jews could not tolerate Jesus going against their established religion. Jesus had to suffer crucifixion because he did not toe the line of Jewish thinking.

Baba remained in hiding from the public eye. He knew full well that once he was known for his miracles, he too would have to suffer. He was therefore against his publicity. He was not happy with his publicity and showed his displeasure even to Sri KM Munshi, who was a Governor of Uttar Pradesh and a devotee to have praised him in one of his articles.

Baba said that if people came to know that he was capable of taking them out of suffering, the world at large would surround him and cut him to pieces to make a garland around their necks to end their sufferings.

Baba therefore worked silently during his lifetime.

Today when he is not in his flesh and bones Baba is more accessible to those who need him through worship of Hanuman. I once spoke to a lady, who lives in Delhi and is a devotee about how and when she met Baba. She told me that she was worshipping Hanuman for some years and sometime at the end of December 2017 she came to know about Baba through face book. Baba came to her vision in dreams. One day on Makar Sankranti day in January 2018, a Sadhu came to her house. The Sadhu told her that he was coming from Hardwar and wanted a new blanket from her. The lady went inside her house but there was no new blanket. She told the Sadhu that since there were no new blankets, he should come again. The Sadhu left. After the Sadhu had left, she realized that he could be no one else but the Baba himself.

I have heard such stories from many other devotees who came to know about Baba after he had left his physical body. Baba has been seen by many devotees even after he left his physical body.

The point that I want to make is that Baba is still working on his devotees or those who worship Hanuman.

Divine souls like Neem Karoli Baba are givers and not hoarders. They share their joy by giving and help the devotees to understand the joy of sharing. That is Seva or service to others.

Neem Karoli Baba gave love in abundance and shared his joy with whosoever came in his contact. He never allowed anybody to leave without giving sumptuous eatables "Prasad."

Neem Karoli Baba is a divine energy.

His divine energy is still present when he is not in human form.

He came and embraced the world through his Leela.

But the leela goes on and would go for ever.

But this can be felt and not seen.

And it can be felt only by those who are capable of receiving his grace.

Or he can be felt only by those whom he pulls through his magnetic force.

While in human body, he was attracted only by those whom he pulled. They instantly felt his divine energy, became attracted and became his devotees, not disciples.

I want to emphasize here the difference between a disciple and a devotee.

A disciple is a learner. A devotee does not have to learn anymore. He has reached the goal through divine grace.

Neem Karoli Baba was an incarnation of divine energy. He did not preach, did not create any organization around him. He lived a very simple life, "love everyone and serve others was his message."

Those who came in touch with him were instantly transformed through his divine energy which is available even now in his Ashram where he lived. Those who pray with devotion are heard even now after he left his physical body.

Such stories appear unbelievable. That was the reason why Baba did not want any publicity of such stories. These are very personal experiences of his devotees who were always scared to tell it publicly.

Those interested to know more about Baba's miracles should read the book "Adbhut Yatharth" (in Hindi) or "Divine Reality" (In English) by Sri Ravi Prakash Pandey and "Miracles of Love" by Ram Dass, the American devotee of Baba.

4
Tulsidas, Rama and Hanuman

As already mentioned in the previous chapters, both Rama and Hanuman are divine incarnations.

I have described earlier the difference between a "Sat Guru" or a Master and divine incarnations.

Masters provide guidance to disciples for spiritual growth. Their spoken words are collected in the form of scriptures.

But incarnations don't give discourses or guidance for growth. Their life itself is a divine play or "Leela." Those, who are lucky enough to be connected with divine incarnations to receive their grace, instantly, become devotees, not disciples. These devotees then describe the "Leela" or divine plays of incarnations in books that are called epics. Epics are not scriptures; epics are descriptions of events in the lives of divine incarnations

Neem Karoli Baba also did not make any disciples. He did not give religious discourses. The only books that are available are from his devotees who collected Baba's divine plays or "Leela." Not much is known about Baba's life.

Divine plays are known as "Lila." The divine play of Rama is called "Rama-lila," that of Krishna "Krishna-Lila" and "Raas-lila."

These plays are enacted in the form of drama in India. "Ram-lila" is very popular in India and has been enacted in the form of drama year after year down the centuries.

Epics and Puranas are the description of "Leelas" Epics and Puranas are the description of "Leelas." For example, "Ramayana" or "Ramcharit Manas" is a description of the divine plays of Lord Rama. "Bhagavata Purana" is a description of the divine plays of Lord Krishna.

In the previous chapters, I have briefly discussed about both the epics in India viz. Ramayana and Mahabharata containing Sri mad Bhagvat Gita.

Ramayana and Rama Charit Manas move around Rama who is the 7th incarnation of God Vishnu. Ram was born in Treta Yuga.

Krishna is the 8th incarnation of God Vishnu. He was born in Dwapar Yuga.

Out of these two epics, Ramayana, especially its Hindi version Ram Charit Manas is most revered among the common masses in India.

The reason why Srimad M. Bhagvat Gita or Ramayana written by Valmiki could not receive support from the common people in India was that these were written in Sanskrit. Sanskrit was not the language of the masses.

Enlightened masters like Buddha and Mahavira also did not speak in Sanskrit. Both of them spoke in the language of the masses. Thus religions around both of them were born and spread in India. Thus religions around both of them were born in India because the message was delivered in the language of the common people.

The story of Rama and Ravana is the story of divine energy versus destructive energy.

Ram Charit Manas is a story of God and his devotee Hanuman.

Rama is an incarnation of God. Hanuman is his devotee.

A devotee derives his energy from God. Hanuman derived his energy from Rama.

Hanuman could do miracles through the divine energy of Rama.

Neem Karoli Baba was also a devotee of Rama. He was an incarnation of Hanuman.

He could do miracles to his devotees and helped to solve mundane problems. His miracles were only to help people understand the divine powers and to develop trust in God. Baba was concerned with mundane problems of man.

Mundane problems in this world eat away our vitality. Meditation gives us silence. But when we are faced with mundane problems, there is disturbance in mind caused by fear of uncertainties.

In meditation, one has to accept the situation without any rationalization. But when one is faced with trivial situations in life, mind begins to rationalize. It does not accept the situation. One is asked to simply watch the situation with awareness.

On the contrary, in prayer one surrenders his worry and anxiety to a deity or god. Surrendering needs no rationalization. One simply surrenders to the divine will and miracle happens. One is free from worries and anxieties.

Baba inspired trust in Hanuman through his miracles and infused confidence that Hanuman also comes to rescue his devotees who are in Sankat (trouble) due to mundane problems.

That was the reason for Baba establishing temples of Hanuman so that trust could develop that there is really someone to look for support when negative energies surround you and make your life hopeless.

There is a saying that:

'सबसे भले वह मूढ़ जिन्हें न व्यापे जगत गति'

(Sabse bhale wai moorha jinhai na vyaapai jagat jad)

Those who are idiots are the best because they remain unaffected by the worldly miseries. They don't suffer. For them there is no need for any prayer or meditation.

Only those, who are sensitive by nature, suffer.

Those who remain steady in intellect know how to rationalize through logic and reason; therefore, they remain unaffected until logic and reason fail to provide relief. The real search begins when all the logic fails to provide relief.

Ravana is a symbol of an intellectual person. He has no heart. He is an "Asur," an egoist.

Today this planet is full of "Aasuric" or devilish energy.

In such times, there is need for divine energies to incarnate on this planet, establish devotion and and prayer to help sensitive humans from negative energies.

Man is hungry for love. Love is the greatest healer. One looks for love with family, friend's relatives. But love is fast disappearing from this planet. Therefore, there is an urgent need to revive divine love on this planet. Ramcharitmanas is a story of love. Neem Karoli Baba is an epitome of love.

This is "Kaliyug" the last epoch or age of the four cycles.

Now this planet is on the verge of destruction through negative forces. Therefore, this planet needs support of divine energy.

Ram Charit Manas points to a truth through the mythology of Rama.

Rama and Hanuman can be true saviors for this planet. They should be seen as universal gods instead of only Hindu gods.

Neem Karoli Baba revived the spirit of devotion and prayer without distinction of nations, caste, creed and religions.

Ram Charit Manas was created by Goswami Tulsidas at a time when India was being invaded by Muslim rulers who came from foreign lands. They tried to eradicate the spirit of prayer and devotion in India which had been established through ages. These outside forces were intolerant and did not respect the feelings of the inhabitants of this land. They killed, murdered, became rulers and destroyed statues, idols, temples and religious places. This was fanaticism.

Although India is today free from the foreign rulers and is called a secular country but the politics of religion is still dominating the nation. This is unfortunate.

Tulsidas wrote Ram Charit Manas in Awadhi, the language of the masses in north India. The earlier version "Ramayana" written by Valmiki was in Sanskrit and therefore could not find acceptance by the masses because of the contrains of Sanskrit language.

It was a bold spirit of Tulsidas that enabled him to write Ram Charit Manas at a time when India was being attacked and invaded by foreign rulers who were trying to establish dynastic rule in India through mass conversions and killings of faiths.

There is another reason why Ram Charit Manas could find acceptance in India whereas Srimad Bhagvat Gita by Krishna could not find acceptance by the masses.

It was because Srimad Bhagvat Gita was the path of Yoga.

Devotion was only mentioned as a passing reference.

Arjuna was not a devotee. He was also not a disciple.

On the contrary, Meera, who had never seen Krishna in physical form, became a devotee of Krishna without ever having read Srimad Bhagvat Gita. A devotee does not need much learning like a disciple. A disciple is a learner.

Learning is a conscious phenomenon. Once learning is complete, it becomes part of the sub – consciousness. A devotee is a heart – oriented person.

It may be difficult for a western reader to know about the terms 'disciple' and 'devotee.' It is because in none of the religions born in the west the concept of Master and Disciple or God and Devotee has existed. The prayers offered in a Church or a Mosque or even a Hindu temple is only ritualistic, born out of tradition, which cannot be called true devotion and prayer. Prayer is individual and not born out of a belief.

For a western seeker, it is difficult to understand why Ramkrishna Paramhans, during prayers, danced and wept before Kali, and went into trance. He was a devotee of deity Ma Kali. Prayer is connected with heart and feeling, and not thinking.

I would like to say something more about Ramkrishna Paramhans. I started my journey through him and was fascinated because he is an unusual saint.

He travelled the path of different religions and came to the conclusion that they reach to the same goal. The difference in religions is only in the boats at the beginning of the journey, but they all reach to the same destination at the end.

Ramkrishna had visions of Ma Kali. Thereafter he worshipped Rama with the attitude of Hanuman. He had visions of Rama and Sita.

Ramkrishna also practised Tantra Sadhana and Vedanta. He was also initiated into Islam. He also started practice of Christianity. He had a vision of Jesus. This is a rare example in the history of spirituality in India.

Ramakrishna regarded the Supreme Being to be both Personal and Impersonal, active and inactive.

He used to say,"when I think of the Supreme Being as inactive – neither creating nor preserving nor destroying – I call Him Brahman or Purusha, the Impersonal God. When I think of Him as active – creating, preserving and destroying – I call Him Shakti or Maya or Prakriti, the Personal God. But the distinction between them does not mean a difference. The Personal and Impersonal are the same thing, like milk and its whiteness, the diamond and its luster, the snake and its wriggling motion. It is impossible to conceive of the one without the other. The Divine Mother and Brahman are one."

In India chanting, singing and prayer in a group helps in raising the energy level. Krishna Das who is an American and a devotee of Neem Karoli Baba is going around the world with chanting and prayer in the western world. Those who participate in chanting, singing and dancing the devotional prayer experience the uplifting t of their energy in groups.

Details of Krishna Das programs around the world can be found on his website http://krishnadas.com/.

It is necessary that such spirit of prayer, chanting, music, dance is revived around the world and western seekers become aware about the concept of divine incarnations. Without coming from head to heart, prayer cannot happen.

That is the purpose of this book.

For the benefit of western readers, I would now like to describe about Tulsidas, Ram Charit Manas, Sunder Kand and Hanuman Chalisa.

Like Tulsidas, Neem Karoli Baba also revived the spirit of Rama and Hanuman by reciting "Sita – Ram, Sita – Ram," Sunderkand and Hanuman Chalisa

Tulsidas

I would like to discuss about Goswami Tulsidas without whom the mythology of Rama and Hanuman would not have found recognition in this age of Kaliyug.

Tulsidas has brought back to life Rama and Hanuman who belong to the Treta Yuga. The love and devotion for Rama and Hanuman cannot be known without the works of Goswami Tulsidas to the common masses.

Rama lives in the hearts of millions of Indians because of Tulsidas. He wrote the epic Ram Charit Manas in the language comprehensible to the masses. Ramayana was earlier written by Valmiki in Sanskrit, which was not the language of the masses; it was a language of the aristocrats.

As already mentioned, Buddha and Mahavira also spoke in Pali and Prakrit language. That is why they could be understood by the common people. That was the reason why religions could be born through both of them in India. The Vedas and Upanishads were also written in Sanskrit language and were not understood by the masses. It remained limited to the Brahmins or the intellectual class only.

Tulsidas (1511–1623) is said to be an incarnation of Maharshi Valmiki who wrote Ramayana in Sanskrit.

Tulsidas spent most of his life in the city of Varanasi. The Tulasi Ghat on the Ganges River in Varanasi is named after him. He founded the Sankatamochana Temple dedicated to Hanuman ji in Varanasi, believed to stand at the place where he had the sight of Hanuman ji.

Tulsidas hints at several places in his works that he had met face to face with Hanuman and Rama.

Tulsidas is a devotee and a seeker through "Sagun Upasana."

As per Tulsidas, the Nirguna Brahman (impersonal God) and Saguna Brahman (personal God with qualities) are one and the same.

"(अगुन सगुन दुइ ब्रहम सरूपा। अकथ अगाध अनादि अनूपा॥)."

"It is the devotion (Bhakti) of the devotee that forces the Nirguna Brahman which is quality-less, formless, invisible and unborn, to become Saguna Brahman with qualities."

Tulsidas gives the simile of a lake – the Nirguna Brahman is like the lake with just water, while the Saguna Brahman is a lake resplendent with blooming lotuses.

Therefore, Saguna Upasana (God with a form) is full of fragrance unlike Nirgun Upasana which is just "dry bones."

At the beginning of the Ramcharitmanas, there is a section devoted to the veneration of the name of Rama.

As per Tulsidas, repeating the name of Rama is the only means to attain to God in the Kali age. The means suited for other ages like meditation, Yoga, and Puja are ineffective in Kali Yuga.

In the first chapter of Ram Charit Manas called "Bal Kand" Tulsidas writes:

"चहुँ जुग तीनि काल तिहुँ लोका। भए नाम जपि जीव बिसोका॥
बेद पुरान संत मत एहू। सकल सुकृत फल राम सनेहू॥
ध्यानु प्रथम जुग मखबिधि दूजें। द्वापर परितोषत प्रभु पूजें॥
कलि केवल मल मूल मलीना। पाप पयोनिधि जन मन मीना॥

नाम कामतरु काल कराला। सुमिरत समन सकल जग जाला।।
राम नाम कलि अभिमत दाता। हित परलोक लोक पितु माता।।
नहिं कलि करम न भगति बिबेकू। राम नाम अवलंबन एकू।।
कालनेमि कलि कपट निधानू। नाम सुमति समरथ हनुमानू।।"

The meaning of above verses is that during Sat Yuga, which is the first epoch or age according to Hindu mythology, meditation or "Dhyana" was the way to attain to God. Satyuga was the age when there was balance in the society, man was simple, there was plenty to eat and to survive, not much worry or anxiety in the society. This was the period when Upanishads were born in India; seers meditated and attained liberation through meditation.

The second age after Sat Yuga was Treta Yuga.

During the Treta Yuga, there were three Avatars of Vishnu – the fifth, sixth and seventh incarnations as Vaaman, Parashurama and Rama respectively.

During the Treta Yuga, the power of humans diminishes slightly, wars break out frequently.

Despite these seemingly negative effects, the Treta Yuga also brought knowledge. This knowledge allowed humans to understand the forces of nature and the true nature of the universe.

The hallmark of this era was the rise of evil in the form of the demon king of Lanka, Ravana.

Lord Vishnu incarnated himself as the son of King Dasharatha and was named Rama.

During Treta Yuga, Yajna was being performed for awakening of spiritual consciousness.

Yajna literally means "sacrifice, devotion, worship, offering.

All spiritual practices initially developed as symbolic and metaphorical but degenerated into rituals at a later stage when priests became the middlemen between a devotee and God.

For example, in a Yajna, fire was worshipped. Fire was symbolic of rising consciousness. The flames of fire rise upwards which symbolically means rising of consciousness. The nature's energies are raw and go downwards or gravitate. For example, sex, hate, anger, lust etc are raw energies, which diminish consciousness. On the contrary, yajna raises the consciousness upwards. During a Yajna, symbolically agricultural seeds such as wheat are put into the fire. These are representative of human raw energies and ego in seed form which should be burnt early in the process of development.

During Treta Yuga, Yajna was the method of worship.

Then comes dwapar age, which is the third out of four Yugas, or ages

In this era, the divine intellect ceases to exist.

People perform other penances when they suffer.

In Kaliyug (present age), Hindus believe that human civilization degenerates spiritually during the Kali Yuga, which is referred to as the Dark Age because in it people are as far away as possible from God.

Tulsidas in the above verse says that in Kaliyug, neither meditation, nor Yajna, nor penances and sacrifices will work; only reciting the name of Rama and Hanuman is enough.

In his view, the name of Rama is greater than both Nirguna and Saguna aspects of God.

He holds that name of Rama is superior to all other names of God,

Neem Karoli Baba was also emphasizing that name of Rama is greater than Rama.

At several places in Tulsidas' works, Rama is seen to be higher than Vishnu and not as an avatar of Vishnu, which is the general portrayal of Rama.

In the Sundarkand, Hanuman tells Ravana that Brahma, Vishnu and Shiva can create, preserve and destroy by the might of Rama.

As per Tulsidas, Rama is not only an avatar, but also the source of avatars – Krishna is also an Avatar of Rama. Thus, Tulsidas clearly considers Rama as supreme Nirgun Brahman and not only an avatar of Vishnu.

In several verses of the Ramcharitmanas, Tulsidas says that the animate and inanimate world is a manifestation of Rama, and the universe is the cosmic form of Rama.

Why is the name of Rama more important than Rama?

In India "Naam (name) and "Rupa" have been considered as constituent processes of the human being: Nama is typically considered to refer to psychological elements of the human person, while rūpa refers to the physical.

Nāma is the Sanskrit term for "name." Spiritually, it is the principal method or tool of meditation, which is meant to unite the individual soul with the Supreme Soul.

It is believed that God existed before the creation of the universe. The name of God is therefore beyond the language structure created by mankind. The Nāma meaning the name is the internal rhythm, the internal sound that a man experiences, the true name of God, and thus ultimate Japa, as it is called in Hinduism or Jaap in Sikhism.

Neem Karoli Baba gave the names of his devotees ending with the word "Das." He gave the names like Hanuman Das, Bhagwan Das, Ram Dass, Krishna Das, and Keshav Das etc. Das means a servant or a devotee. It means one who is in service of God.

Neem Karoli Baba revived the faith in Tulsidas, Ram Charit Manas, Hanuman Chalisa, Sundarkand and Rama and Hanuman.

As already mentioned, man is very weak in the times of crisis. Therefore, a support is needed in such moments.

Human beings have their own problems and worries; therefore they cannot provide any support except to offer sympathy.

Sympathy does not solve the crisis.

Therefore, a deity for support is required. Normally a man would not believe in the existence of invisible deities or gods. Man believes only that is accessible to the eyes, ears and other sensory organs.

Therefore, one has to first understand that there is a world beyond our senses. We can all feel vibrations that soothe us as well as those that hurt us. The positive and negative energies can be felt.

The purpose of prayer is to invoke these invisible vibrations to support us to come out of our negativity. Once we are uplifted through divine energies, we become receivers of such energies and our negativity gradually vanishes.

Tulsidas had the sight of Rama in Chitrakoot.

'Darshan' of Rama to Tulsidas was that of a child who pasted sandalwood on the forehead of Tulsidas.

Such Darshan of Neem Karoli Baba have also been reported by Baba's devotees. He is reported to have given Darshan in different forms even after leaving his body.

Tulsidas is also attributed to have performed miracles. In one such miracle, he is reported to have brought back a Brahmin to life.

In another miracle, the emperor of Delhi, Akbar summoned Tulsidas on hearing of his bringing back a dead man to life.

Tulsidas declined to go but he was later forcibly brought before Akbar and was asked to perform a miracle. Tulsidas declined by saying, "It's a lie, all I know is Rama." The emperor imprisoned Tulsidas at Fatehpur Sikri.

Tulsidas refused to bow to Akbar and recited Hanuman Chalisa for forty days.

Suddenly an army of monkeys descended upon the town and wrecked havoc in all corners of Fatehpur Sikri, entering each home and the emperor's harem, scratching people and throwing bricks from ramparts.

An old Hafiz told the emperor that this was the miracle of the imprisoned Fakir.

The emperor fell at Tulsidas' feet, released him and apologized. Tulsidas stopped the menace of monkeys and asked the emperor to abandon the place.

The emperor agreed and moved back to Delhi. Ever since Akbar became a close friend of Tulsidas and he also ordered a firman that followers of Lord Rama, Lord Hanuman and other Hindus, should not be harassed in his kingdom.

In the Vikram Samvat 1631 (corresponding to CE 1574), Tulsidas started composing Ram Charit Manas in Ayodhya. The epic was composed in about 2 years and seven months.

Tulsidas in composing Ram Charit Manas is very humble and begins by praying to all the deities, saints and even sinners.

Ram Charit Manas

Ram Charit Manas is considered to be the greatest epic in Hindi literature. It is poetry. Poetry cannot be translated in prose because it arises out of feeling and not thinking.

Let us try to understand the metaphorical meaning of Ram Charit Manas.

As already mentioned earlier, the episode of Rama happened in Treta Yuga. In Treta Yuga, which followed Sat Yug, the demonic forces were on the rise. In every age, according to Hinduism, there is a decline in values; the ultimate decline is in the current age called Kaliyug.

The war is always between heart – oriented and intellect – oriented society.

It is a left brain versus right brain phenomenon.

The right brain is represented by heart. Music, painting, sculpture is a heart phenomenon. Compassion and empathy happens only in sensitive hearts. Intellect is a left brain phenomenon. It is oriented towards logic and thinking. It strengthens the ego.

Rama incarnated on this planet to crush the demonic forces. Rama represented the divinity, Ravana was the demon king. The war was between divine forces versus demonic forces. Ultimately, the divine forces were victorious.

While reading Ram Charit Manas, one is surprised to note that the army of Rama consisted of animals such as monkeys, bear, and eagle etc. It was not an army of men.

Those were the days when plants, birds, animals and human beings were living in harmony. The animals and plants are sensitive to vibrations. They understand the difference between a friend and foe through subtle vibrations.

Even in Christianity, there is a story of Saint Francis of Assisi. One day, while Francis was traveling with some companions, they happened to come upon a place to the road where birds filled the trees on either side. Francis told his companions to "wait for me while I go to preach to my sisters the birds." The birds surrounded him, intrigued by the power of his voice, and not one of them flew away. He is often portrayed with a bird, typically in his hand. In another incidence, St Francis calmed down a ferocious wolf that was a menace to the town.

Even Neem Karoli Baba was seen amongst snakes and tigers who sat quietly beside him.

Hanuman who is a central character in Ram Charit Manas was a monkey God. He was in service of Rama. Without him, the story of Rama winning over Ravana would not be complete.

In modern times, man has become inimical to plants, birds and animals. The civilization that has developed in mega cities by cutting plants, by destroying forests, killing sea animals for food has created much ecological imbalance. That is why this planet is facing a disaster.

But in this age of Kaliyug, it is not possible for divine incarnations to fight a war with demonic forces. The nuclear weapons have given great destructive power to demonic forces. Therefore, the divine forces are only trying to change the people through love and transforming their hearts. The devotees of Baba are an example of selfless service to humanity. Dr. Larry Brilliant of America is an example of selfless service to mankind through eradication of small pox and establishing Seva foundation. This was initiated at the behest of Neem Karoli Baba who was able to look into the future of Dr. Brilliant. The incidences written by Ram Dass in "Miracles of Love" are also expressions of feelings and not of intellect.

Ram Charit Manas is an epic written by a heart – oriented person like Tulasi Das. It is difficult to translate feelings. One would have to visualize the characters and the situations through heart to be able to feel the episode. Feelings are often inexpressible. Feelings can be best expressed through tears and not words.

If you read Ram Charit Manas, you will be surprised to note the kind of love that existed in the kingdom of Ayodhya where Rama was born. When Rama was asked to go in exile for 14 years and his brother Bharat was asked to occupy the throne, he declined. In Kaliyug there is a continuous struggle and killings to occupy the position of power. Brothers kill each other to grab power. It looks surprising why Bharat refused to occupy the throne and waited for 14 long years for Rama to return to Ayodhya. Sita and Lakshman also accompanied Rama in exile.

Love existed amongst human beings and animals.

In today's' age, family ties are breaking up, respect and love is diminishing. I personally feel that Ram Charit Manas should be read worldwide to know how love, respect and devotion amongst family members and society can raise the divine energy on this planet.

On the contrary, in the kingdom of Ravana there was no love between Ravana and his younger brother Vibhishan. Terror persisted in the entire kingdom. These were demonic forces.

In today's world, terror persists all over the globe. Warfare has assumed another dimension of economic war. It is no longer necessary to invade a nation for economic gains. Economic war is killing human beings all over the world. In communist countries, there is terror all over. Human rights are ignored blatantly.

I cannot express the feelings of Ram Charit Manas but would like to narrate it like a story as briefly as possible for a western reader not well – versed in understanding the feelings of the characters.

Ram Charit Manas consists of seven Kandas or episodes.

The first two parts, Bāl Kāṇḍ (Childhood Episode) and Ayodhyā Kāṇḍ (Ayodhya Episode), make up more than half of the work. The other parts are Araṇya Kāṇḍ (Forest Episode), Kiśkindhā Kāṇḍ (Kishkindha Episode), Sundar Kāṇḍ (Pleasant Episode), Laṅkā Kāṇḍ (Lanka Episode), and Uttar Kāṇḍ (Later Episode). I would like to briefly discuss about the episodes for the benefit of western readers not familiar with Ram Charit Manas.

- **Bāl Kāṇḍ (Childhood Episode)**

The primary message is that Rama incarnated on earth to protect the righteous who follow the path of Dharma.

In this episode, Tulsidas praises Dashrath, Rama's father who is the king of Ayodhya. He also narrates about the three queens of Dashrath viz, Kaushalya, Kaikeyi and Sumitra.

Kaushalya gives birth to Rama who is the eldest of all.

Kaikeyi gives birth to Bharat.

Sumitra gives birth to Lakshman and Shatrughna.

The story then moves to the birth of Ravana, the demon king and his brothers.

King Janak arranges a Swayamvar ceremony (where a bride had the choice to choose her groom) for the wedding of his daughter Sita.

A great bow of Shiva is placed in the arena. There are many princes including Rama and Lakshman in this ceremony. The condition is that whosoever shall break the bow of Shiva shall be married to Sita.

Finally, Rama breaks the bow and Sita is married to Rama.

Rama weds Sita

After the wedding Sita and Rama return to Ayodhya where there was a great celebration and rejoicing.

- **Ayodhyā Kāṇḍ (Ayodhya Episode)**

As king Dashrath was getting old, he wanted his eldest son to be enthroned.

The second wife of the king, Kaikeyi was not happy at this decision of the king. She wanted her son Bharat to be the king.

She reminds king of the two boons given to her earlier and in return demanded that Bharat be enthroned and Rama be sent in exile for 14 years.

Queen Kaikeyi is unmoved by Dashratha's lamentations and finally the king emotionally breaks down.

The pain of separation from Rama is too much for Dashrath who passes away crying Rama's name.

Rama accepts his stepmother's bidding and decides to leave the kingdom. Sita and Lakshman also leave along with Rama.

Rama, Sita and Lakshman moving into exile

Bharat is away during all these happenings. He is not in Ayodhya and is not aware of the move made by his mother.

Bharat is greatly pained and blames himself for Rama leaving Ayodhya. He accuses his mother of bringing ruin to the family.

Bharat cannot bear the thought of sitting on the throne with his father dead and his brothers in exile in the forest.

The cremation of King Dashrath takes place. Bharat and Shatrughna decide to go into the forest and ask Rama to return to Ayodhya and take the throne.

Despite all of Bharat's convincing, Rama is true to the word given to his father and step – mother Kaikeyi, and vows that he will fulfill her wish.

Bharat says that he simply cannot sit on the throne while Rama wanders in the forest. He asks Rama for his sandals, which he would place at the throne and would only act as Rama's representative and not as a full-fledged king. With much sorrow and hurt, Bharat leaves Rama and returns to Ayodhya. He decides that he would not live in the capital of the kingdom while Rama is in exile and so lives like a hermit in a nearby town called Nandigram.

- **Araṇya Kāṇḍ (The Forest Episode)**

The story takes a new turn, as Rama, Sita and Lakshman are approached by the sister of the demon-king Ravana, called Surpanakha. She immediately takes a liking for Rama and falls in love with him. She disguises herself and talks to Rama in sweet tones. Rama rejects her advances. She then approaches Lakshman.

However, Lakshman also rejects her advances.

Surpanakha takes it as a great insult to be spurned like this, and attempts to hurt Sita. Lakshman takes hold of his sword and chops off Surpanakha's ear lobes and nose.

Feeling humiliated, Surpanakha leaves the forest and goes to the abode of her cousins Khara, Dooshan and Trishira. They are angry at the treatment meted out to their sister and leave with the intention of killing Rama. However, all of them along with their army of fourteen thousand demons are annihilalted by Rama single-handedly.

Surpanakha is greatly upset and visits Ravana at his residence in Lanka. She explains all that has happened, after which Ravana calls for his old friend Maricha. Ravana hatches a plot and asks Maricha to disguise himself as a golden deer to lure Sita, so that Ravana may then kidnap her . Maricha has already felt the power of Rama and is apprehensive; however, he thinks that he is going to die either way since Ravana will kill him in rage for refusing him.

Ravana and Marich immediately leave for Rama's forest abode. Maricha takes his position and instantly Sita is attracted by his golden form. Rama knows Ravana's intentions and orders Sita to place her shadow (Maya Sita) in her place, while she would hide in the fire.

She asks Rama time and again to hunt the deer and bring its skin to her. Rama runs after the deer and is soon quite far away from the ashram. Rama releases an arrow and hits the deer. Impersonating Rama's voice, Marich shouts out to Lakshman to help him.

Maya Sita (hereafter called simply Sita) hears the cry and orders Lakshman to go to help his brother.

Ravana, while posing as a begging minstrel, uses this opportunity to forcibly kidnap Sita from the ashram.

Ravana kidnapping Sita

Jatayu, the great vulture, sees Ravana's sinful act and attempts to fight with him, but Ravana has too much power and cuts off Jatayu's wings and leaves him for dead.

Rama and Lakshman return to find the ashram empty. They anxiously set out to find Sita and find the severely wounded Jatayu.

Jatayu dies in Rama's lap and attains liberation.

The brothers then head towards the Pampasarovar Lake.

Kiśkindhā Kāṇḍ (The Kiśkindhā Region Episode)

Sugriva sees Rama and Lakshman at the foothills of the high Rishyamuk mountains.

He consults Hanuman as to whether he thinks they have been sent by his brother Bali.

Hanuman disguises himself as a Brahmin and approaches the brothers. Hanuman recognizes the true nature of Rama as God-incarnation and surrenders himself to his Holy feet.

He tells the brothers that his king, Sugriva wishes to extend his friendship to them and will help them to find Sita.

Rama asks Sugriva why he resides in the mountains instead of Kishkindha, whereupon Sugriva tells of his feud with his brother Bali.

Rama sympathizes with Sugriva and decides to help Sugriva in return for the latter's help in finding Sita.

Ram kills Bali and installs Sugriva as king of Kishkindha and Angada, Bali's son, as prince regent.

Rama kills Bali

Sugriva becomes too attached to his new regal lifestyle and forgets about his promise to Rama, which fills Rama with great anger. Rama asks Lakshman to bring Sugriva to him. Lakshman enters the royal court and threatens to burn the entire city to ashes.

Sugriva is gravely worried and asks Hanuman to pacify him. Lakshman escorts Sugriva to Rama and upon seeing Him, Sugriva falls as His feet and begs forgiveness.

Sugriva immediately orders the gathering of the region's bear and monkey community. Armies of bears and monkeys are dispatched north, south, east and west to search for Sita. Rama knew that only Hanuman was really capable of finding Sita. He asks Hanuman to narrate the agony of separation from her and then hands over his ring. Hanuman is joined by Angad, Nala, Kesari and Jambavan and many others as they head towards the south. As the army approaches the coast, Jambavan and Angad see a cave by the shore of the ocean. The cave is occupied by Sampati (who is actually Jatayu's older brother). There is a conversation during which Angad explains that Jatayu died serving Rama and thereafter Sampati narrates his biography. He tells the monkeys that he is sure that Sita is captive in Ashok Vatika in Lanka. The island is 800 miles away and requires someone who is able to jump the distance. Jambavan deduces that Hanuman is the only one capable of the task.

"कहइ रीछपति सुनु हनुमाना। का चुप साधि रहेहु बलवाना।।
पवन तनय बल पवन समाना। बुधि बिबेक बिग्यान निधाना।।
कवन सो काज कठिन जग माहीं। जो नहिं होइ तात तुम्ह पाहीं।।
राम काज लगि तब अवतारा। सुनतहिं भयउ पर्वताकारा।।"

"Kahai rīchapati sunu hanumānā. Kā chup sādhi rahēhu balavānā..

Pavana tanaya bala pavana samānā. budhi bibēka bigyāna nidhānā..

Kavana sō kāja kaṭhina jaga māhīṃ. Jō nahiṃ hōi tāta tumha pāhīṃ"

The above verse is about the power of Hanuman. He was accursed that until he is told about his power, he shall not become aware of it. Jambavan in this verse tells Hanuman that he has immense power, there is nothing difficult for him to attain in this world. Having heard it, Hanuman became like a mountain and remembered that he was born to serve Rama.

Sunder Kāṇḍ (The Pleasant Episode)

Hanuman takes Jambavan's suggestion and immediately takes off for Lanka.

Hanuman takes a minute form and, remembering Rama, enters Lanka.

Hanuman flies through the various palaces and gardens for his search of Sita, and amongst all the demonic activities going on in Lanka, Hanuman sees a palace where Sri Hari's name is being chanted.

He is drawn towards the palace and decides to visit the inhabitant.

The palace belongs to Ravana's brother, Vibhishan.

Hanuman narrates Rama katha (story) and then introduces himself. Hanuman proceeds to Ashok Vatika where he finally sees Sita.

Hanuman meets Ma Sita in Ashok Vatika, Lanka

He positions himself on a branch of a tree, under which Sita was sitting, and contemplates his next move.

He sees Ravana walk towards Sita and beg her to glance at least once toward him.

She simply looks at a blade of grass to insult him.

Ravana threatens to behead Sita but is calmed down by his wife, Mandodari.

Hanuman has to use all his powers of calm not to react to Ravana's threats.

When all is quiet again, Hanuman begins to sing the glory of Rama in sweet tones.

He then approaches Sita and explains who he is.

He presents the ring lord Rama had given him and Sita is overjoyed.

She blesses Hanuman with many kind words and boons.

Hanuman tells Sita that he is hungry and asks for her permission to eat fruits from the grove. He not only eats but manages to destroy large parts of it. He easily kills one of Ravana's sons, prince Aksaya. Indrajit arrives in the grove and Hanuman allows himself to be captured. He is brought in front of the king of Lanka, Ravana. Ravana orders his death, however, Vibhishan reminds him that Hanuman is an envoy and cannot be killed according to religious principle. Ravana decides to humiliate Hanuman by setting his tail on fire. Large amounts of clothes are tied to his tail and soaked in oil. Hanuman chants the name of Rama and his tail begins to get longer, and more cloth and oil is used. He changes from his small form into a gigantic form and decides to torch alight the whole of Lanka.

He returns to the ocean to extinguish his tail and then goes to Sita to reassure her that the next time she sees him, it will be with Rama. He bids farewell to Sita and leaps back towards Angad and Jambavan. The monkey army then ventures back to where Sugriva, Rama and Lakshman are waiting. On arrival Hanuman explains all that happened and immediately an army is prepared to go south towards Lanka.

Meanwhile, in Lanka, both Mandodari and Vibhishan counsel Ravana to hand Sita back to Rama. Ravana takes great exception to this suggestion and begins to insult Vibhishan particularly. He tells him he has no need for a weakling like him and that he is no longer needed. Vibhishan decides to join Rama who was already on way to Lanka. Vibhishan falls at Rama's feet and begs him for protection. The army deliberates over how to cross the ocean to Lanka. The deity of the seas tells Rama of the boon obtained by the monkey brothers Nila and Nala, and that they have the power to build a bridge to link the seashore to Lanka.

- **Laṅkā Kāṇḍ (The Lanka Episode)**

Nala and Nila building the bridge across the sea

Jambavan asks the monkeys Nala and Nila to begin work on building the bridge across the sea.

Rama remembers Lord Shiva and decides to install a shrine for Rameswaram. Upon completion, the army of Rama begins to cross the bridge and arrives at Lanka, taking camp on Mount Suvela. Ravana hears of the advances of Rama's army and feels greatly agitated. Mandodari asks Ravana to return Sita to Rama as she fears for her husband's life. Ravana is dismissive of Rama's power and pacifies his wife. Next, Ravana's son Prahasta attempts to reinforce his mother's sentiments, but all to no avail.

Rama fires a warning shot from his retreat in Suvela. The arrow strikes Ravana's crown and royal umbrella. Mandodari once again attempts to convince Ravana of handing Sita back to Rama. Meanwhile, Rama asks Jambavan what should be done. Jambavan suggests that they send Angada, as messenger, to give Ravana a chance to return Sita. On reaching Ravana's court, Angada explains he is the ambassador of Rama, and tells Ravana that he still has time to save himself from destruction. Ravana insults Angada and his refusal to comply makes war inevitable.

The war begins with great ferocity as Ravana loses half of his army on the first day itself. Indrajit, Ravana's son, is required to enter the battle far earlier than he expected. He severely wounds Lakshman with his special weapon, the Saang. Hanumanji is ordered to fetch the doctor of Lanka called Sushena. Sushena tells Rama that there exists an herb called Sanjivani which can only be found in the Himalayan Mountains. It is the only hope to save Lakshman. Hanuman immediately reassures Rama that he shall find this herb. As Hanuman is about to leave, Ravana orders the demon Kalanemi to impede him. However, Hanuman kills Kalanemi with ease. Hanuman reaches the mountain but can't find the herb. In his frustration, he decides to take the entire mountain to Lanka.

Hanuman bringing the herb from Himalaya to save Lakshman

Hanuman makes good speed towards Lanka when suddenly he is shot by an arrow as he approaches Nandigram. Hanuman is mistaken to be a demon by Bharat. Hanuman falls to the ground together with the great hill. Hanuman regains consciousness and recognizes that Bharat is Rama's brother. He continues on to Lanka where he delivers the Sanjivani herb and Sushena treats Lakshman. Rama embraces Hanuman with great pride and affection. Ravana takes the news of Lakshman's recovery very badly and decides to awaken his brother Kumbhakarna. Kumbhakarna kills indiscriminately and wreaks much havoc. Rama releases an arrow which kills him instantly. The death of his brother scares Ravana greatly. Indrajit hastily tries to arrange a ceremony to receive great boons and powers but is interrupted by Hanuman and Angada. Lakshman takes up arms against Indrajit and kills him. Rama throws numerous arrows at Ravana but is unable to kill him. He asks Vibhishan as to how to kill his brother after which Rama finally kills Ravana. The war is over.

Ravana's funeral takes place and Vibhishan is crowned the king of Lanka. Hanuman carries the happy news to Sita in Ashok vatika. Finally Rama and Sita are reunited. Rama and the army prepare to depart from Lanka and return to Ayodhya. Rama, Sita, Lakshman and the senior monkeys travel back in Ravana's flying vehicle, Pushpak Vimaan.

- **Uttar Kānd (The Epilogue)**

Rama returns to Ayodhya after serving his exile. Bharat is anxious that his brother still hasn't arrived. Hanuman meets Bharat telling him of the arrival of Rama, Sita and Lakshman. Bharat rushes to Ayodhya to tell the citizens of the great news. As the Pushpak Vimaan landed in Ayodhya the citizens shouted chants of 'Glory be to Ramchandra.' Rama, Sita and Lakshman collectively touch the feet of the sage Vashishta on arriving in Ayodhya and thereafter greet all that have gathered in the assembly. Lastly, Rama meets Bharata with great affection and love. Rama's coronation takes place and he is finally crowned king of Ayodhya.

Rama's coronation in Ayodhya

Above is a brief of Ram Charit Manas for a western seeker.

Hanuman is a central character in the entire episode. The fifth episode "Sundar Kand" gives an account of the strength of Hanuman and of how he serves Rama with devotion.

I would, therefore, like to dwell upon this fifth episode once again for the sake of a western seeker.

Rama's coronation in Ayodhya

Above is a brief of Ram Charit Manas for a western seeker.

Hanuman is a central character in the entire episode. The fifth episode "Sunder Kand" gives an account of strength of Hanuman and how he serves Rama with devotion.

I would therefore like to dwell upon this fifth episode once again for the sake of a western seeker.

Sunder Kand

Sunder Kand is the fifth episode in Ram Charit Manas. It is important because without this episode it was difficult to locate Ma Sita who was living in exile in Lanka.

Sunder Kand is recited by religious Hindus, preferably on Tuesdays or Saturdays, these days having been earmarked for special prayers to Hanuman.

Sunderkand describes relationship between a devotee and his master. A true devotee is dedicated in a self less service for the master.

Neem Karoli Baba who is also an incarnation of Hanuman never made disciples. He only made devotees.

A devotee like Larry Brilliant who came to India as a hippie came in contact with Baba. He received his divine energy and became a devotee. Larry worked with great devotion to save mankind from a deadly disease. He is a true devotee who did a selfless service for the mankind.

It is difficult to describe the feelings of a devotee. The western disciples of Baba are true devotees because they did not come with any previous background of spirituality in India. The Indian devotees on the contrary have a background of a master and disciple and Gurus. Many Indians also are devotees of Baba but I consider western devotees more dedicated to rendering service out of a feeling towards the suffering. This service by Baba's devotees is different from the service rendered by Christian missionaries.

Hanuman is an ideal devotee of Rama. His devotion to Rama brings great energy to him to perform tasks unimaginable. His service is self-fulfilling, not for any reward.

Hanuman has been blessed by Ma Sita and Rama to live on this planet until the end of this age of Kaliyug. Anyone who is a devotee of Rama becomes a devotee of lord Hanuman and is shielded from worries.

Hanuman meets Rama in the last year of the latter's 14-year exile, after the demon king Ravana had kidnapped Sita. With his brother Lakshman, Rama is searching for his wife Sita. This, and related Rama legends are the most extensive stories about Hanuman.

I would also like to mention that Hanuman has many names.

Other names of Hanuman include:

- Anjaneya meaning "the son of Hanuman's mother Anjana";
- Kesari Nandan, based on his father, which means "son of Kesari"
- Maruti or the son of the wind god;
- Bajrang Bali, "the strong one (Bali), who had limbs (anga) as hard as a vajra (bajra)";
- Sankata Mochana, the remover of calamities (sankata)

Hanuman does not have a real name. He is nameless. The names mentioned above are only the attributes of Hanuman.

Likewise Neem Karoli Baba is not the real name of Baba. He is also called by different names and finally known as Maharajji or Babaji.

There is a great similarity between Hanuman and Neem Karoli Baba.

Both never worked for name and fame. Both have helped devotees to come out of worries or mundane problems.

Neem Karoli Baba as an incarnation of Hanuman revived the spirit of Hanuman in the modern age.

In India there are more temples of Hanuman than any other deity. People have great trust in Hanuman. They are rescued from mundane problems. Hanuman can be pleased very easily unlike other gods and deities.

Sandarac Kanda is the only chapter of the *Ramayana* in which the hero is not Rama, but rather Hanuman. The work depicts the adventures of Hanuman and his selflessness, strength, and devotion to Rama are emphasized in the text. Hanuman was fondly called "Sandarac" by his mother Anjani and Sage Valmiki chose this name over others as the Sandarac Kanda is about Hanuman's journey to Lanka.

Hanuman has many attributes:

Chiranjivi (immortal): Hanuman is blessed to be immortal. He will be a part of humanity forever, while the story of Rama lives on;

Kurūp and Sundar: he is described in Hindu texts as kurūp (ugly) on the outside, but divinely sundar (beautiful inside);

Kama-rupin: He can become smaller than the smallest, larger than the largest adversary at will. He uses this attribute to shrink and enter Lanka, as he searches for the kidnapped Sita imprisoned in Lanka. Later on, he takes on the size of a mountain, blazing with radiance, to show his true power to Sita;

Strength: Hanuman is extraordinarily strong, one capable of lifting and carrying any burden for a cause. He is called Vira, Mahavira, Mahabala and by other names signifying this attribute of his. During the epic war between Rama and Ravana, Rama's brother Lakshman is wounded. He can only be healed and his death prevented by an herb found in a particular Himalayan mountain. Hanuman leaps and finds the mountain. There, states Ramayana, Hanuman finds the mountain is full of many herbs. He doesn't know which one to take. So, he lifts the entire Himalayan Mountain and carries it across India to Lanka for Lakshman. His immense strength thus helps Lakshman recover from his wound. This legend is the popular basis for the iconography where he is shown flying and carrying a mountain on his palm;

Innovative: Hanuman is described as someone who constantly faces very difficult odds, where the adversary or circumstances threaten his mission with certain defeat and his very existence. Yet he finds an innovative way to turn the odds. For example, after he finds Sita, delivers Rama's message, and persuades her that he is indeed Rama's true messenger; he is discovered by the prison guards. They arrest Hanuman, and under Ravana's orders take him to a public execution. There, the Ravana's guards begin his torture, tie his tail with oiled cloth and put it on fire. Hanuman then leaps, jumps from one palace rooftop to another, thus burning everything down;

Bhakti: Hanuman is presented as the exemplary devotee (*bhakta*) of Rama and Sita. The Hindu texts such as the *Bhagavata Purana*, the *Bhakta Mala*, the *Ananda Ramayana* and the *Ramcharitmanas* present him as someone who is talented, strong, brave and spiritually devoted to Rama.

The Rama stories such as the *Ramayana* and the *Ramcharitmanas*, in turn themselves, present the Hindu dharmic concept of the ideal, virtuous and compassionate man (Rama) and woman (Sita) thereby providing the context for attributes assigned therein for Hanuman;

Learned Yogi: In the late medieval texts and thereafter, such as those by Tulsidas, attributes of Hanuman include learned in Vedanta philosophy of Hinduism, the Vedas, a poet, a polymath, a grammarian, a singer and musician par excellence

Remover of obstacles: in devotional literature, Hanuman is the remover of difficulties or "Sankat Mochan";

Hanuman Chalisa

Tulsidas wrote *Hanuman Chalisa*, a devotional song dedicated to Hanuman. He claimed to have visions where he met face to face with Hanuman.

The Hanuman Chalisa literally means forty verses or "chaupais" on Hanuman. It is a Hindu devotional hymn (stotra) addressed to Lord Hanuman and is the best known text apart from the Ramcharitmanas. The word "chālīsā" is derived from "chālīs," which means the number forty in Hindi, as the Hanuman Chalisa has 40 verses (excluding the couplets at the beginning and at the end).

Hanuman Chalisa is a devotional hymn dedicated to Lord Hanuman.

For the western seeker, I reproduce Hanuman Chalisa verses and their English translation as below:

Shri Guru Charan Saroj Raj	After cleansing the mirror of my mind with the pollen
Nij man mukur sudhari	dust of holy Guru's Lotus feet. I profess the pure,
Varnau Raghuvar Vimal Jas	untainted glory of Shri Raghuvar, which bestows the four–
Jo dayaku phal chari	fold fruits of life(Dharma, Artha, Kama and Moksha).

Buddhi Hin Tanu Janikai	Fully aware of the deficiency of my intelligence, I
Sumiraun Pavan Kumar	concentrate my attention on Pavan Kumar and humbly
Bal budhi Vidya dehu mohi	ask for strength, intelligence and true knowledge to
Harahu Kalesa Vikar	relieve me of all blemishes, causing pain.
Jai Hanuman gyan gun sagar	Victory to thee, O' Hanuman! Ocean of Wisdom-All
Jai Kapis tihun lok ujagar	hail to you O'Kapisa! (fountain-head of power, wisdom and Shiva-Shakti) You illuminate all the three worlds (Entire cosmos) with your glory.
Ram doot atulit bal dhama	You are the divine messenger of Shri Ram, the
Anjani-putra Pavan sut nama	repository of immeasurable strength, though known only as Son of Pavan (Wind), born of Anjani.
Mahavir Vikram Bajrangi	With Limbs as sturdy as Vajra (The mace of God Indra)
Kumati nivar sumati Ke sangi	you are valiant and brave. On you attends good Sense and Wisdom. You dispel the darkness of evil thoughts.
Kanchan varan viraj subesa	Your physique is beautiful, golden coloured and your dress
Kanan Kundal Kunchit Kesa	is pretty. You wear ear rings and have long curly hair.
Hath Vajra Aur Dhvaja Virajai	You carry in your hand a lightning bolt along with a victory
Kandhe moonj janeu sajai	(kesari) flag and wear the sacred thread on your shoulder.
Sankar suvan kesri Nandan	As a descendant of Lord Sankar, you are a comfort and pride

Tej pratap maha jag vandan	of Shri Kesari. With the lustre of your Vast Sway, you are propitiated all over the universe.
Vidyavan guni ati chatur	You are the repository of learning, virtuous and fully accom–
Ram kaj karibe ko aatur	plished, always keen to carry out the behest of Shri Rama.
Prabhu charitra sunibe ko rasiya	You are an ardent listener, always so keen to listen to the
Ram Lakhan Sita man Basiya	narration of Shri Rama's Life Stories. Your heart is filled with what Shri Rama stood for. You therefore always dwell in the hearts of Shri Rama, Lakshman and Sita.
Sukshma roop dhari Siyahi dikhava	You appeared before Sita in a diminutive form and spoke to
Vikat roop dhari lanka jarava	her in humility. You assumed an awesome form and struck terror by setting Lanka on fire.
Bhima roop dhari asur sanghare	With over-whelming might you destroyed the Asuras
Ramachandra ke kaj sanvare	(demons) and performed all tasks assigned to you by Shri Rama with great skill.
Laye Sajivan Lakhan Jiyaye	You brought Sanjivan (A herb that revives life) and restored
Shri Raghuvir Harashi ur laye	Lakshman back to life, Shri Raghuvir (Shri Rama) cheerfully embraced you with his heart full of joy.
Raghupati Kinhi bahut badai	Shri Raghupati (Shri Rama) lustily extolled your excellence and

Tum mam priya Bharatahi sam bhai	said: "You are as dear to me as my own brother Bharat."
Sahas badan tumharo yash gaavain	Thousands of living beings are chanting hymns of your glories;
Us kahi Shripati kanth lagaavain	saying thus, Shri Ram warmly hugged him (Shri Hanuman).
	(In Hindu mythology, "Sahas-badan" is the name of Shesh-naag,
	The Serpent with a thousand hoods)
Sankadik Brahmadi Muneesa	When the sages like Sanaka, even Lord Brahma,
Narad Sarad sahit Aheesa	the great hermit Narad himself, Goddess Saraswati and Ahisha, the lord of serpents i.e. Shesh-naag)
Yam Kuber Digpal Jahan te	Even Yamraj (God of Death) Kuber (God of Wealth) and the
Kavi kovid kahi sake kahan te	Digpals (deputies guarding the four corners of the Universe)
	have been vying with one another in offering homage to your
	glories. How, then, can a mere poet give adequate expression
	to your super excellence.
Tum upkar Sugreevahin keenha	You rendered a great service to Sugreeva. You united him with
Ram milaye rajpad deenha	Shri Ram and he installed him on the royal throne. By heeding
Tumharo mantra Vibheeshan mana	your advice, Vibhishan became Lord of Lanka. This is known
Lankeshwar Bhaye Sub jag jana	all over the Universe.
Yug sahastra jojan par Bhanu	On your own you dashed upon the Sun, which is at a fabulous

Leelyo tahi madhur phal janu	distance of two thousand yojans (one yojan is equal to eight miles), thinking it to be a sweet luscious fruit.
Prabhu mudrika meli mukh mahee	Carrying the Lord's Signet Ring in your mouth, there is
Jaladhi langhi gaye achraj nahee	little wonder that you easily leapt across the ocean.
Durgaam kaj jagat ke jete	The burden of all difficult tasks of the world become light
Sugam anugraha tumhre tete	with your kind grace.
Ram duare tum rakhvare,	You are the sentry at the door of Shri Ram's Divine Abode.
Hota na agya binu paisare	No one can enter it without your permission,
Sub sukh lahahi tumhari sarna	All comforts of the world lie at your feet. The devotees enjoy all
Tum rakshak kahu ko dar na	divine pleasures and feel fearless under your benign Protection.
Aapan tej samharau aapai	You alone are befitted to carry your own splendid valour. All the
Teenhau lok hank te kanpai	three worlds (entire universe) tremor at your thunderous call.
Bhoot pisach Nikat nahin aavain	All the ghosts, demons and evil forces keep away with the
Mahavir jab naam sunavain	sheer mention of your great name, O'Mahaveer!!
Nasai rog harai sab peera	All diseases, pain and suffering disappear on reciting regularly
Japat nirantar Hanumant veera	Shri Hanuman's holy name.
Sankat se Hanuman chudavai	Those who remember Shri Hanuman in thought, words and deeds

Man Karam Vachan dhyan jo lavai	with Sincerity and Faith, are rescued from all crises in life.
Sub par Ram tapasvee raja	All who hail, worship and have faith in Shri Ram as the Supreme
Tin ke kaj sakal Tum saja	Lord and the Penance Incarnate. You make all their difficult tasks very easy.
Aur manorath jo koi lavai	Whosoever comes to you for fulfillment of any desire with faith
Soi amit jeevan phal pavai	and sincerity, Will he alone secure the imperishable fruit of human life.
Charon Yug partap tumhara	All through the four ages your magnificent glory is acclaimed far
Hai persiddh jagat ujiyara	and wide. Your fame is radiantly acclaimed all over the Cosmos.
Sadhu Sant ke tum Rakhware	You are the Saviour and the guardian angel of Saints and Sages and
Asur nikandan Ram dulare	Destroyer of all demons. You are the darling of Shri Ram.
Ashta sidhi nav nidhi kai data	You can grant to any one, any yogic power of Eight Siddhis
Us var deenh Janaki mata	(power to become light and heavy at will) and Nine Nidhis (Riches, comfort, power, prestige, fame, sweet relationship etc.) This boon has been conferred upon you by Mother Janaki.
Ram rasayan tumhare pasa	You possess the power of devotion to Shri Ram. In all rebirths

Sada raho Raghupati ke dasa	you will always remain Shri Raghupati's most dedicated servant.
Tumhare bhajan Ram ko pavai	Through hymns sung in devotion to you, one can find Shri Ram
Janam janam ke dukh bisravai	and become free from sufferings of several births.
Ant kaal Raghuvir pur jayee	If at the time of death one enters the Divine Abode of Shri Ram,
Jahan janam Hari-Bakht Kahayee	thereafter, in all future births he is born as the Lord's devotee.
Aur Devta Chitta na dharahi	One need not entertain any other deity for Propitiation, as
Hanumat seyi sarve sukh karahi	devotion of Shri Hanuman alone can give all happiness.
Sankat kate mite sab peera	One, who remembers Sri Hanuman, the mightiest of the mighty, is freed from all the sufferings and ill-fated contingencies of
Jo sumirai Hanumat Balveera	rebirths in the world.
Jai Jai Jai Hanuman Gosain	Hail, Hail, Hail, Shri Hanuman, Lord of senses. Let your victory
Kripa Karahu Gurudev ki naayin	over the evil be firm and final. Bless me in the capacity as my supreme guru (teacher).
Jo sat bar path kar koi	One, who recites this Chalisa one hundred times, becomes free from the
Chhootahi bandh maha sukh hoi	bondage of life and death and enjoys the highest bliss at last.
Jo yah padhai Hanuman Chalisa	One, who recite Hanuman Chalisa (The forty Chaupais)
Hoya siddhi sakhi Gaureesa	Regularly, is sure to be benefited. Such is the evidence of no less a witness as Bhagwan Shankar.

Tulsidas sada hari chera	Tulsidas as a bonded slave of the Divine Master, stays perpetually at
Keejai nath Hriday mahi dera	his feet and prays "Oh Lord! You enshrine within my heart ."
Pavantnai sankat haran,	Oh! conqueror of the Wind, Destroyer of all miseries, you are a
Mangal murti roop.	symbol of Auspiciousness.
Ram Lakhan Sita sahit,	Along with Shri Ram, Lakshman and Sita, reside in my heart.
Hridaye basahu sur bhoop.	Oh! King of gods.

I would like to mention for the benefit of a western reader to first become familiar with "Sundarkand" before reading "Hanuman Chalisa."

Sundarkand gives account of the entire service that Hanuman performed for Rama and the entire team.

Hanuman Chalisa is a summary of service that Hanuman performed. It is a praise of Hanuman.

Hanuman is said to be more pleased with the recitation of 'Sundarkand" because it focuses on Lord Rama and Ma Sita.

The western reader may also like to download APP through playstore called "Ramayana." This is a TV serial on Ramayana with subtitles in English, which was very popular in India during the eighties.

It is indeed necessary to revive the spirit of devotion and prayer throughout the world through a universal god "Hanuman." The foundation has been laid by Goswami Tulsidas and Neem Karoli Baba.

Only Hanuman can save this planet from demonic forces, which are on the rise during the last about 300 years after the society became industrial from the previous agricultural society.

5
Quality of Life on Planet Earth and Need for a Universal God

For a large part of my life I worked as a Quality Professional.

While working in the field of quality my main concern was quality assurance of product and service quality. Later on the concept was expanded to Quality Management of organizations and to Total Quality Management. The field of management standards was further expanded to Environmental Management & Occupational Health & Safety Management. Today there is a plethora of management standards developed by national and international standards organizations.

But no standards have been developed for quality of life on this planet. In my view, every human activity should ultimately culminate in improving the quality of life on earth.

The definition of "quality" has been changing over time. Even today some variance is found in how it is described.

Joseph M. Juran who is considered the international quality Guru defined quality of product as which meets customer needs leading to customer satisfaction.

The international standard ISO 9000 defines quality as "The totality of features and characteristics of a product or service that bear on its ability to satisfy stated or implied needs.

Customer satisfaction is the ability of the product or service to meet their needs and expectations.

Today organizations are competing with each other to create more and more expectations from the customers to survive in the market.

Organizations try to innovate and create more and more desires and expectations for their customers.

By creating desires, the human society is moving more and more towards materialistic life.

Quality of life can be defined as that which brings a blissful life on this planet.

But materialistic life based upon creating and fulfilling desires does not provide a blissful life.

Buddha defined bliss as a state of non-misery.

Material comforts do provide happiness, comfort and pleasure. But that is only one side of the story. Hidden underneath pleasure is pain. Both are part of the same coin, one is visible, the other is hidden underneath.

Buddha says "desire is misery."

Neem Karoli Baba also said, "If you want to see God, kill desires. Desires are in the mind. When you have a desire for something, don't act on it and it will go away. If you desire to drink this cup of tea, don't, and the desire for it will go away."

Killing desires does not mean "to starve." One should understand desire and transcend desire. Buddha's don't mean suppression of desires.

The consumerism and materialism in the world is growing because organizations are creating more and more desires in the human beings through science and technology.

Spirituality seeks happiness within; Materialism seeks happiness without. Spirituality teaches us to aspire for a better life, a more illumined life. Materialism teaches us to desire more material goods and material wealth... Spirituality takes the help of material progress but is never a slave to materialistic desires.

There is nothing wrong in material advancement. What is required is that material advancement should function as a servant and spiritual growth should remain the master.

The west is spiritually poor, materially rich. The east is materially poor, spiritually rich. But both are half and both are suffering.

Let us try to analyze the scientific development on this planet in the last 300 years and how it has brought misery on this planet.

Science brought industrial revolution. With the advancement of technology, the war methods also changed. The traditional war changed and saw the emergence of missile war and nuclear bomb.

Countries were forced to buy war weapons to safeguard their boundaries. This entailed huge expenditure even by the third world countries where millions are living below the poverty line.

To fight war money was needed. Monarchs and Kings needed money to expand territories or to safeguard boundaries against enemies to remain in power. This gave rise to money lenders who funded wars. They lent money to governments through a complex banking system. Central banks controlled by private people came into existence. The first such bank was Bank of England.

Money lending continues unabated till today. Through money control these private people have not only controlled the governments, their elected representatives, but the entire assets of a nation, media and created a debt based economy. These are hidden faces of devils on this planet. They can be called demonic forces or "Asurs" of the Treta Yuga.

To combat these demonic forces with the traditional war fought by Lord Rama or Lord Krishna is not possible today. These demonic forces have nuclear weapons and missiles and other destructive weapons to destroy the planet.

Now these forces have created a new kind of war called "Economic War."

What is the way out for a common man to safeguard against these demonic forces?

It is only by invoking divine energies and by accepting a universal God that one can be saved.

Without such a universal God, this planet is doomed to perish.

With the growth of science, logic and reason, the western philosopher Nietzsche proclaimed that trust in God was vanishing.

He is said to have quoted" He who fights with monsters might take care lest he thereby become a monster. And if you gaze for long into an abyss, the abyss gazes also into you"

This is a very powerful statement. It means if you take revenge with someone you would imbibe the same quality as that of the offender.

It is natural to react when someone abuses you. The law of cause and effect works. Is it possible to transcend this law?

The law which transcends the law of cause and effect is called law of freedom. It is simply freedom. This is what in Hinduism is called "Moksha." One is free from the law of cause and effect. Hindus call it the law of Karma.

But freedom comes only when a higher energy than that provided by nature comes into play. One is in bondage till one remains under the influence of laws of nature. With the support of divine energy, which is a higher energy one is lifted from the laws of gravitation.

But Nietzsche did not provide any prescription for safeguarding against monster.

Bible says, "But I say unto you, that ye resist not evil: but whosoever shall smite thee on thy right cheek; turn to him the other also"

The statement of Bible is against the law of cause and effect. It can happen only when one has transcended law of cause and effect and has become free of the natural instincts. No prescription is given in Bible to achieve such a state of freedom.

Since with the growth of science, logic and reason, Christian God became a subject matter of doubt, Nietzsche simply declared that "God is dead." This was the beginning of the western existentialism. It laid the foundation of a Godless universe. Universe became mechanical without any intelligence. Without a God man became free. This was beginning of anxiety, worry, despair and angst.

Prior to industrial revolution, the society was by and large agrarian. Man was fulfilling the needs from land, ploughing the field for agriculture. Man was dependent on the animals, taking care of animals and plants. Animals were in the service of man. Life was not materialistic. Man lived with nature. There was plenty of forest land, the nature's resources hidden under the earth had still not been exploited, and environment was clean with greenery all around.

Since there was no mechanization, manual work was the only way of producing goods.

Amongst the tribal communities such a life can still be seen. Culture has still not penetrated amongst tribals.

About 300 years ago the civilization took a turn. Science was developing which brought industrial age over a period of time. This was an industrial revolution.

I would like to trace the reasons for decline in trust in God since the advent of industrial revolution and development in science.

The industrial revolution can be seen in three stages.

First Industrial Revolution

The Industrial Revolution was the transition to new manufacturing processes during the period from about 1760 to 1820–1840. This transition included going from hand production methods to machines, new chemical manufacturing and iron production processes, the increasing use of steam power, the development of machine tools and the rise of the factory system.

First Industrial Revolution

The Industrial Revolution began in Great Britain, and many of the technological innovations were of British origin. By the mid-18th century Britain was the world's leading commercial nation, controlling a global trading empire with colonies in North America and Africa, and with some political influence on the Indian subcontinent, through the activities of the East India Company. The development of trade and the rise of business were major causes of the Industrial Revolution.

The Industrial Revolution marks a major turning point in history; almost every aspect of daily life was influenced in some way or the other. In particular, average income and population began to exhibit unprecedented sustained growth. Some economists say that the major impact of the Industrial Revolution was that the standard of living of the general population began to rise consistently for the first time in history, although others have said that it did not begin to meaningfully improve until the late 19th and 20th centuries.

The First Industrial Revolution, which ended in the early to mid 1800s, was punctuated by a slowdown before the Second Industrial Revolution in 1870,, though a number of its characteristic events can be traced to earlier innovations in manufacturing, such as the establishment of a machine tool industry, the development of methods for manufacturing interchangeable parts and the invention of the Bessemer Process to produce steel,

Second Industrial Revolution

The Second Industrial Revolution, also known as the Technological Revolution, was a phase of rapid industrialization in the final third of the 19th century and the beginning of the 20th.

The Second Industrial Revolution is generally dated between 1870 and 1914 (the start of World War I).

The enormous expansion of rail and telegraph lines after 1870 allowed unprecedented movement of people and ideas, which culminated in a new wave of globalization. In the same period, new technological systems were introduced, most significantly electrical power and telephones. The Second Industrial Revolution continued into the 20th century with early factory electrification and the production line, and ended at the start of World War I.

The rapid expansion of telegraph networks took place throughout the century. The Atlantic Telegraph Company was formed in London in 1856 to undertake construction of a commercial telegraph cable across the Atlantic Ocean.

The telephone was patented in 1876 by Alexander Graham Bell, and like the early telegraph, it was used mainly to speed business transactions.

Alexander Graham Bell patents the telephone.

One of the most important scientific advancements in all of history was the unification of light, electricity and magnetism through Maxwell's electromagnetic theory. A scientific understanding of electricity was necessary for the development of efficient electric generators, motors and transformers. Heinrich Hertz demonstrated and confirmed the phenomenon of electromagnetic waves that had been predicted by Maxwell.

It was Italian inventor Guglielmo Marconi, who successfully commercialized radio at the turn of the century. He founded The Wireless Telegraph & Signal Company in Britain in 1897 and in the same year transmitted Morse code, the first ever wireless communication over open sea, and made the first transatlantic transmission in 1901.

The key development of the vacuum tube in 1904 underpinned the development of modern electronics and radio broadcasting. Subsequent invention of the triode allowed the amplification of electronic signals, which paved the way for radio broadcasting in the 1920s.

The period from 1870 to 1890 saw the greatest increase in economic growth in such a short period as ever in previous history. Living standards improved significantly in the newly industrialized countries as the prices of goods fell dramatically due to the increase in productivity. This caused unemployment and great upheavals in commerce and industry, with many laborers being displaced by machines and many factories, ships and other forms of fixed capital becoming obsolete in a very short time span.

Like the first industrial revolution, the second one supported population growth and saw most governments protect their national economies with tariffs. The wide-ranging social impact of both the revolutions included the remaking of the working class as new technologies appeared. The changes resulted in the creation of a larger, increasingly professional middle class, the decline of child labor and the dramatic growth of a consumer-based material culture.

Third Industrial Revolution

The Digital Revolution, also known as the Third Industrial Revolution, is the shift from mechanical and analogue electronic technology to digital electronics, which began anywhere from the late 1950s to the late 1970s with the adoption and proliferation of digital computers and digital record keeping that continues to the present day. Implicitly, the term also refers to the sweeping changes brought about by digital computing and communication technology during (and after) the latter half of the 20th century. Analogous to the Agricultural Revolution and Industrial Revolution, the Digital Revolution marked the beginning of the Information Age.

Digital Revolution

Central to this revolution is the mass production and widespread use of digital logic circuits, and its derived technologies, including the computer, digital cellular phone, and the Internet. These technological innovations have transformed traditional production and business techniques.

The economic impact of the digital revolution has been large. Without the World Wide Web (WWW), for example, globalization and outsourcing would not be nearly as feasible as they are today. The digital revolution radically changed the way individuals and companies interact. Small regional companies were suddenly given access to much larger markets. Concepts such as On-demand services and manufacturing and rapidly dropping technology costs made possible innovations in all aspects of industry and everyday life.

After initial concerns of an IT productivity paradox, evidence is mounting that digital technologies have significantly increased the productivity and performance of businesses.

Impact of Industrial Revolutions on War

Industrialization played a major role in World War 1. It allowed for new machinery to be produced and at a much faster rate than ever before… There were many new weapons found to World War 1 that increased the deadliness of war.

At the beginning of the Industrial Revolution, armies fought on foot or on horse, with swords, lances or muzzle-loading muskets. The musket was a long gun, firing round balls of lead.

Industrial warfare is a period in the history of warfare ranging roughly from the early 19th century and the start of the Industrial Revolution to the beginning of the Atomic Age, which saw the rise of nation-states, capable of creating and equipping large armies, navies, and air forces, through the process of industrialization.

Warfare using Tanks

The era featured mass-conscripted armies, rapid transportation (first on railroads, then by sea and air), telegraph and wireless communications, and the concept of total war. In terms of technology, this era saw the rise of rifled breech-loading infantry weapons capable of high rates of fire, high-velocity breech-loading artillery, chemical weapons, armored warfare, metal warships, submarines, and aircraft.

There are several reasons for the rise of total warfare in the 19th (?) century. The main one is industrialization. As countries' capital and natural resources grew, it became clear that some forms of warfare demanded more resources than others. Consequently, the greater cost of warfare became evident. The use of nuclear weapons first came into being during the last months of WW II, with the dropping of atomic bombs on Hiroshima and Nagasaki. This was the only use of nuclear weapons in combat. For a decade after World War II, the United States and later the Soviet Union (and to a lesser extent the United Kingdom and France) developed and maintained a strategic force of bombers that would be able to attack any potential aggressor from bases inside their countries.

Before the development of a capable strategic missile force in the Soviet Union, much of the war-fighting doctrine held by western nations revolved around the use of a large number of smaller nuclear weapons used in a tactical role. It is arguable if such use could be considered "limited," however, because it was believed that the US would use their own strategic weapons (mainly bombers at the time) should the USSR deploy any kind of nuclear weapon against civilian targets.

A revolution in thinking occurred with the introduction of the intercontinental ballistic missile (ICBM), which the Soviet Union first successfully tested in the late 1950s. To deliver a warhead to a target, a missile was far less expensive than a bomber that could do the same job. Moreover, at the time it was impossible to intercept ICBMs due to their high altitude and speed.

Intercontinental Missiles

In the 1960s, another major shift in nuclear doctrine occurred with the development of the submarine-based nuclear missile (SLBM). It was hailed by military theorists as a weapon that would assure that a surprise attack would not destroy the capability to retaliate, and therefore would make nuclear war less likely.

Hydrogen Bomb

The Cold War

After World War II, the United States and the Soviet Union were the world's strongest nations. They were called superpowers. They had different ideas about economics and government. They fought a war of ideas called the Cold War… The Soviet Union won control of Eastern Europe.

The Cold War got its name because both sides were afraid of fighting each other directly. In a "hot war," nuclear weapons might destroy everything.

Cold War

During 1989 and 1990, the Berlin Wall came down; borders opened, and free elections ousted Communist regimes everywhere in Eastern Europe. In late 1991 the Soviet Union itself dissolved into its component republics. With stunning speed, the Iron Curtain was lifted and the Cold War came to an end.

Economic War

The concept of economic warfare is most applicable to conflict between nation states, especially in times of total war, which involves not only the armed forces of an enemy nation but also mobilization of that nation's entire economy towards the war effort. In such a situation, causing damage to the enemy's economy during 1989 and 1990, the Berlin Wall came down, borders opened, and free elections ousted Communist regimes everywhere in Eastern Europe. In late 1991 the Soviet Union itself dissolved into its component republics. With stunning speed, the Iron Curtain was lifted and the Cold War came to an end. Policies and measures in economic warfare may include blockade, blacklisting, preclusive purchasing, rewards and the capturing or control of enemy assets or supply lines.

Banking System and Control of Money

At the dawn of humanity, bartering was used in lieu of **money** to buy goods. As early man began to rear domestic livestock, one of the earliest forms of barters included cattle, sheep as well as vegetables and grain.

But barter system had to change and money had to be invented to facilitate as a medium of exchange.

After all, the person who has what you need might not need what you have to trade. Money solves that problem neatly. Real value comes with each exchange, and everyone gaining from the convenience. The idea is really inspired, which might explain why so many diverse minds came up with it.

Money Changers

History records that the money – changers have used every form of abuse, intrigue, deceit, and violent means possible to maintain their control over governments by controlling money and its issuance.

Jesus was so upset by the sight of money – changers in the temple that he waded in and started to tip over the tables and drive them out with a whip, and this being the one and only time we ever hear of him using force during his entire ministry.

So what caused Jesus to become so aggressive?

Jesus and the Money – changers

For a long time the Jews had been called upon to pay their temple tax with a special coin called the half – shekel shekel. It was a measured half ounce of pure silver with no image of a pagan emperor on it.

It was to them the only coin acceptable to God.

But because there were only a limited number of these coins in circulation, the money – changers were in a buyer's market and like with anything else in short supply, they were able to raise the price to what the market would bear.

They made huge profits with their monopoly on these coins and turned this time of devotion into a mockery for profit. Jesus saw this as stealing from the people and proclaimed the whole setup to be "a den of thieves."

Once money is accepted as a form of exchange, those who produce, loan out and manipulate the quantity of money are obviously in a very strong position. They were the "Money – changers."

In the medieval England (1000 – 1100 A.D.), goldsmiths started offering to keep other people's gold and silver safe in their vaults, and in return people walking away with a receipt for what they have left there.

These paper receipts soon became popular for trade as they were less heavy to carry around than gold and silver coins.

After a while, the goldsmiths noticed that only a small percentage of their depositors ever came in to demand their gold at any one time. So cleverly the goldsmiths made out some receipts for gold which didn't even exist, and then they loaned it out to earn interest.

Later, they incorporated this practice into the banking system. They even gave it a name to make it seem more acceptable, christening the practice **'Fractional Reserve Banking'** which translates to mean lending out many times more money than you have assets on deposit.

Today banks are allowed to loan out at least ten times the amount they actually are holding, so while you wonder how they get rich charging you 11% interest, it's not 11% a year they make on that amount but actually 110%.

The Bank of England was set up as a privately owned bank through investors buying shares.

Rothschild's

The Rothschild family (who were goldsmiths) pioneered international finance in the early 19th century. The family provided loans to the Bank of England and purchased government bonds in the stock markets. Their wealth has been estimated to possibly be the most in modern history. In 1804, Nathan Mayer Rothschild began to deal on the London stock exchange in financial instruments such as foreign bills and government securities. From 1809 Rothschild began to deal in gold bullion, and developed this as a cornerstone of his business. From 1811 onward, he undertook to transfer money to pay Wellington's troops on campaign in Portugal and Spain against Napoleon, and later to make subsidy payments to British allies when these organized new troops after Napoleon's disastrous Russian campaign. His four brothers helped co-ordinate activities across the continent, and the family developed a network of agents, shippers and couriers to transport gold—and information—across Europe. This private intelligence service enabled Nathan to receive in London the news of Wellington's victory at the Battle of Waterloo a full day ahead of the government's official messengers.

The 13 Satanic Bloodlines that Rule the World – Rothschild's

The Rothschild familiy was instrumental in supporting railway systems across the world and in complex government financing for projects such as the Suez Canal. The family bought up a large proportion of property in Mayfair, London.

The Japanese government approached the London and Paris families for funding during the Russion-Japanese War. The London consortium's issue of Japanese war bonds would total £11.5 million.

From 1919 to 2004 the Rothschild's' Bank in London played a role as epicenter of the gold – fixing.

Paris had emerged as an international center of finance in the mid-19th century, second only to London. It had a strong national bank and numerous aggressive private banks that financed projects all across Europe and the expanding French Empire.

One key development was setting up one of the main branches of the Rothschild family. In 1812, James Mayer Rothschild arrived in Paris from Frankfurt, and set up the bank "De Rothschild Frères." This bank funded Napoleon's return from Elba and became one of the leading banks in European finance. The Rothschild banking family of France funded

France's major wars and colonial expansion. The Banquet de France founded in 1796 helped resolve the financial crisis of 1848 and emerged as a powerful central bank.

Many of these banks are owned by about a dozen European banking organizations, mostly British, and most notably the Rothschild banking dynasty. Through their American agents they were able to select the board of directors for the New York Fed and to direct U.S. monetary policy.

The Rothschild family is a wealthy Jewish family descending from Mayer Amschel Rothschild (1744–1812),

Mayer Amschel Rothschild is credited with being the inventor of modern banking. Many members of the Rothschild family are billionaires, who hold massive fortunes.

Bank of England has been used as a model and now nearly every nation has a Central Bank with fractional reserve banking at its core.

These central banks have the power to take over a nation's economy and become that nation's real governing force. What we have here is a scam of mammoth proportions covering what is actually a hidden tax being collected by private concerns.

The country sells bonds to the bank in return for money it cannot raise in taxes. The bonds are paid for by money produced from thin air. The government pays interest on the money it borrowed by borrowing more money in the same way. There is no way this debt can ever be paid; it has and will continue to increase.

If the government did find a way to pay off the debt, the result would be that there would be no bonds to back the currency, so to pay the debt would be to kill the currency.

"When a government is dependent upon bankers for money, they and not the leaders of the government control the situation, since the hand that gives is above the hand that takes… Money has no motherland; financiers are without patriotism and without decency; their sole object is gain."

For both sides of a war to be loaned money from the same privately owned Central Bank is not unusual. Nothing generates debt like war. A Nation will borrow any amount to win. So naturally, if the loser is kept going to the last straw in a vain hope of winning, then the more resources are used up by the winning side before their victory is obtained, more loans are taken out, more money made by the bankers; and even more amazing, the loans are usually given on condition that the victor pays the debts left by the loser.

The 19th century became known as the age of the Rothschild's when it was estimated that they controlled half of the world's wealth. While their wealth continues to increase today, they have managed to blend into the background, giving an impression that their power has waned. They only apply the Rothschild name to a small fraction of the companies they actually control. Some authors claim that the Rothschild's had not only taken over the Bank of England but they had also in 1816 backed a new privately owned Central Bank in America called The Second Bank of The United States, causing huge problems to the American president.

War uses up more materials more quickly than anything else on earth. In war expensive equipment doesn't wear out slowly, it gets blown up. (It's interesting to note that during the 119 year period from the founding of the Bank of England to Napoleon's defeat at Waterloo, England had been at war for 56 years, while the rest of the time preparing for it. In the process, the money – changers had been getting rich. So there it was, the newly formed Federal Reserve poised to produce any money the U.S. Government might need from thin air with each dollar standing to make a healthy interest.

World War I (1914-1918)

The Germans borrowed money from the German Rothschild's bank, the British from the British Rothschild's bank, and the French from the French Rothschild's.

American super banker J.P. Morgan was, amongst other things, also a sales agent for war materials. Six months into the war, his spending of $10 million a day made him the largest consumer on the planet.

The Rockefeller's and the head of President Wilson's War Industries Board, Bernard Baruch each made some 200 million dollars while families contributed their sons to the bloody front lines, but profit was not the only motive for involvement.

Russia had spoiled the money – changers' plan to split America into two, and remained the last major country not to have its own central bank.

However, three years after the start of the war, the entire Russian Royal Family was killed and Communism began.

The Russian Revolution was also fuelled with British money.

Communism, or more accurately, socialism, is not a movement of the downtrodden masses, but of the economic elite.

Hitler's rise to power was almost completely financed by money drawn from the privately owned American Federal Reserve.

"After WW-I, Germany fell into the hands of the international bankers.

Those bankers bought her and they now own her, lock, stock, and barrel. They have purchased her industries, they have mortgages on her soil, they control her production, and they control all her public utilities.

World War 1

World War II (1939-1945)

World War II saw the US debt increase by 598%, while Japan's debt went up by 1,348%, with France up by 583% and Canada up by 417%.

Adolf Hitler

With the hot war over, the cold war began, the arms race causing more and more borrowing. Now the money changers could really concentrate on global domination.

World Bank and IMF

During the post second world war period and with the introduction of the Breton Woods system in 1944, two organizations were created: the International Monetary Fund (IMF) and the World Bank. Encouraged by these institutions, commercial banks started to lend to sovereign states in the third world. This was at the same time as inflation started to rise in the west. The Gold standard was eventually abandoned in 1971 and a number of banks were caught out and became bankrupt due to third – world country debt defaults.

While the World Bank represents 188 countries, it is run by a small number of economically powerful countries. These countries (which also provide most of the institution's funding) choose the leadership and senior management of the World Bank, and their interests dominate the bank.

The unequal voting power of western countries and the World Bank's role in developing countries makes it a pillar of global apartheid.

The permanent debt of Third World Countries is constantly being increased to provide temporary relief from the poverty being caused by previous borrowing.

So, on a positive note, it's very encouraging to know that the world is waking up and another fact, which some people still enjoy placing in the conspiracy realm, is that a few families, such as the Rothschild's, completely control the World Bank and multiple federal governments. By control, we mean that they basically own the money supply as well as have high ownership in global resources, thus controlling global geo-politics and more.

IMF and World Bank...
Destroying Countries
– Secret Documents Taken Away from IMF-WB –

I've come to an inescapable and profoundly disturbing conclusion. I believe that an elite group of people and the corporations they run have gained control over not just our energy, food supply, education, and healthcare, but also over virtually every aspect of our lives; and they do it by controlling the world of finance, not by creating more value, but by actually controlling the source of money."

"History records that the money – changers have used every form of abuse, intrigue, deceit, and violent means possible to maintain their control over governments by controlling money and its issuance."

The permanent debt of Third World Countries is constantly being increased to provide temporary relief from the poverty being caused by previous borrowing. As world resources continue to be sucked into this insatiable black hole of greed, if allowed to continue the entire world will face a similar fate.

President James Madison said "Without being radical or overly bold, I will tell you that the Third World War has already started – a silent war, not for that reason any the less sinister. This war is tearing down Brazil, Latin America and practically all the Third World. Instead of soldiers dying there are children, instead of millions of wounded there are millions of unemployed; instead of destruction of bridges there is the tearing down of factories, schools, hospitals, and entire economies... It is a war by the United States against the Latin American continent and the Third World. It is a war over the foreign debt, one which has as its main weapon interest, a weapon more deadly than the atom bomb, more shattering than a laser beam."

If a group or organization had used its hard – earned money to help these developing nations, then we might sympathise that there should be a real effort to repay these loans. But the money used was created from fractional reserve banking. The money loaned to the Third World came from the 90% the banks allow themselves to loan on the 10% they actually held. It didn't exist, it was created from nothing, and now people are suffering and dying in an effort to pay it back.

This has gone beyond clever financing, it is wholesale murder and it is time we stopped it.

Most people don't realize that the issuing of money is essentially a private business, and that the privilege of issuing money has been a major bone of contention throughout history.

Wars have been fought and depressions have been caused in the battle over who issues the money; however, the majority of us are not aware of this, and this is largely due to the fact that the winning side became and increasingly continues to be a vital and respected member of our global society, having an influence over large aspects of our lives including our education, our media and our governments.

Major Forces Causing Crisis on this Planet

I have tried to bring out in the preceding paragraphs that the major cause of inequality amongst human beings on this planet is distribution of money.

Both Christianity and Islam have opposed usury or interest on borrowings by a lender.

Some of the earliest known condemnations of usury come from the Vedic texts of India. Similar condemnations are found in religious texts from Buddhism, Judaism, Christianity, and Islam (the term is riba in Arabic and ribbit in Hebrew). At times, many nations from ancient Greece to ancient Rome have outlawed loans with any interest. The Catholic Church in medieval Europe banned the charging of interest at any rate, as well as charging a fee for the use of money.

Despite this opposition by all the religions in the world, the demonic forces thrive on lending money to sovereign states through the central banks, which are privately managed. The entire economy of the world today is a debt – based economy. There is plenty for every human being on this planet in terms of resources, but the control of money by demonic forces does not allow every human being to equally enjoy the available resources.

Therefore, in my view, it is the control of money by a few, charging of interest to money that is lent and creating mortgages on the assets, which are the major causes of human suffering.

Every nation of the world works on the basis of a deficit budget. The revenue that is generated by the sovereign states through taxes goes to repay the borrowings. Further borrowings are sought to meet the expenditure and the cycle goes on. In third world countries, the major component of expenditure is spent in repayment of loans and interest, government expenditure, defense and security expenditure with a meager amount left for the welfare of the population. Inflation keeps on mounting,

This is appalling state of things.

In my view, greed and fear are two major causes that are the root cause of all misery.

Greed promotes accumulation of things and material comforts. Fear brings hatred towards those who may take away these possessions.

Unless we create love towards life, man would suffer.

Love can flower only with love for a God or divine.

Need for a Universal God

During the eighteenth – century Europe, there was an intellectual and philosophical movement in Europe. This was called the age of enlightenment. This was a consequence of scientific revolution. The authority of monarchy and church was challenged which led to political revolutions.

Reason became the primary source of authority. Ideals like liberty, progress, tolerance, fraternity, constitutional government and separation of church and state became the subject of discussion. Absolute monarchy and the fixed dogmas of the Roman Catholic Church were challenged. The Enlightenment was marked by an emphasis on the scientific method and reductionism, along with increased questioning of religious orthodoxy.

Bacon, Descartes, Locke, Spinoza, Beccaria, Diderot, Hume, Kant, Montesquieu, Rousseau, Adam Smith, and Voltaire were some of the pioneers who promoted rational thinking and logic in place of trust and faith in Orthodox Church. Immanuel Kant tried to reconcile rationalism and religious belief.

In 1776, Adam Smith published 'The Wealth of Nations,' often considered the first work on modern economics as it had an immediate impact on British economic policy that continues into the 21st century.

Existentialism

Existentialism asserts that people actually make decisions based on subjective meaning rather than pure rationality. The rejection of reason as the source of meaning is a common theme of existentialist thought, as is the focus on the feelings of anxiety and dread that we feel in the face of our own radical freedom and our awareness of death. Kierkegaard advocated rationality as a means to interact with the objective world (e.g., in the natural sciences), but when it comes to existential problems, reason is insufficient: "Human reason has boundaries."

Søren Kierkegaard and Friedrich Nietzsche were two of the first philosophers considered fundamental to the existentialist movement, though neither used the term "existentialism" and it is unclear whether they would have supported the existentialism of the 20th century. They focused on subjective human experience rather than the objective truths of mathematics and science, which they believed were too detached or observational to truly get at the human experience. They were interested in people's quiet struggle with the apparent meaninglessness of life and the use of diversion to escape from boredom.

Existentialist believes that life has no purpose; individual has to find the purpose. An existential crisis is a moment at which an individual questions if hisr life has meaning, purpose, or value… This issue of the meaning and purpose of human existence is a major focus of the philosophical tradition of existentialism.

Existentialistic ideas came out of a time in society when there was a deep sense of despair following the Great Depression and World War II. There was a spirit of optimism in society that was destroyed by World War II and its mid-century calamities. This despair has been articulated by existentialist philosophers well into the 1970s and continues on to this day as a popular way of thinking and reasoning (with the freedom to choose one's preferred moral belief system and lifestyle).

An existentialist could either be a religious moralist, agnostic relativist, or an amoral atheist. Kierkegaard, a religious philosopher,

Nietzsche, an anti-Christian, Sartre, an atheist, and Camus an atheist, are credited for their works and writings about existentialism. Sartre is noted for bringing the most international attention to existentialism in the 20th century.

Jean-Paul Sartre

Each basically agrees that human life is in no way complete and fully satisfying because of suffering and losses that occur when considering the lack of perfection, power, and control one has over one's life. Even though they do agree that life is not optimally satisfying, it nonetheless has meaning. Existentialism is the search and journey for true self and true personal meaning in life.

Existentialism, Buddha and Hanuman

Friedrich Nietzsche's – God is dead

Quality of Life on Planet Earth and Need for a Universal God | 187

Buddha meditating, doesn't believe in God

Hanuman praying to Lord Rama and Ma Sita

Existentialism, Buddha and Hanuman, all the three are focused on human misery.

Western existentialism denies existence of God. For existentialist "God is dead." Without a God, existentialist does not know the way to come out of misery. He remains in anguish, worry and despair. For him life is meaningless. This despair is accentuated by various wars including the latest war, which is economic war. Existentialist lives in negativity. Various psychosomatic diseases, auto – immune disorders are a result of this negativity for which modern medical science has no solution except to administer anti-depressant drugs.

Buddha also denies a personal God. But for Buddha God is not dead. He trusts God within. By discovering God within, Buddha transcends misery into a state of non-misery called "Anand" or bliss. Buddha attains to love and compassion.

After Buddha died, those who came in contact with Buddha became Bhikkus. They became monks or renunciates. They gave up families and started begging for food. This was a tragedy. Monks, whether Christian monks or Buddhist bhikkus, became escapists. They became burden on the society. All kinds of perversions developed because monks lived a secluded life and enforced celibacy.

Buddhism became a cult. A cult loses its spirit after the master is gone.

Around Hanuman there is no cult. Hanuman is a devotee of Rama.

Rama is an incarnation of God in human form and also a formless God. Hanuman helps those who trust him to solve mundane problems and obstacles so that trust in God can develop.

Buddha does not help to solve mundane problems. Buddha had no mundane problems. He was a prince and lived a luxurious life. He was not after material comforts. He was fully satiated. The only problem that he encountered was death. He wanted to penetrate the mystery of death. Meditation helped him to go within and encounter that which is deathless. Contrary to Hindus who called the deathless, the immortal within as "Atman" or soul, Buddha did not give it a name. He called it Shunyata. He negated Hindus. What Hindus called "Purnata" or fullness, Buddha called "Shunyata" or emptiness. Hindus did not accept Buddha.

Initially those who came in contact with Buddha were princes of those days. But later, when it became a mass movement, it became a religion of beggars and died in spirit.

Neem Karoli Baba as an incarnation of Hanuman works on millions in resolving mundane problems to develop trust in Rama. No cult can exist around Neem Karoli Baba. His emphasis is on recitation of Rama. By reciting the name of Rama one day the trust would arise. Trust is not a prerequisite for recitation of the name 'Rama.'

Rama who incarnated in human form had to leave this planet one day. His form is no longer available. But his name persists. That is why Baba said the name of Rama is bigger than Rama (in form). Forms disappear but name persists.

Human misery is the focus of existentialism, Buddha and Hanuman.

Existentialism has no solution except to live in negativity. Buddha is able to solve the problem of mystery of death by encountering the deathless within through meditation. Hanuman and Neem Karoli Baba do not advocate meditation, renunciation, becoming a monk. They simply help to solve mundane problems to develop trust. That is why Hanuman should be regarded as a universal deity. Hanuman is a deity for the householders. Neem Karoli Baba lived with householders. He was not a renunciate monk.

Meditation requires practice. Osho devised many meditation techniques for the modern man. These meditations last for one hour. It does provide silent moments when one encounters the inner silence. But it does not help to solve worries and anxiety for the remaining twenty three hours. It becomes more like a Sunday prayer in a church.

Prayer and devotion do not require any technique. It is not one – hour affair. You have simply to remember the name of God. That God is Rama whose devotee is Hanuman. Hanuman helps to remove the obstacles arising in the mind due to anxiety and worry. The problems are not necessarily solved but dissolved. With the dissolution of worries one becomes settled. That is the mystery of prayer.

Existentialism and Buddhism, born of different worlds, came to many of the same conclusions. Existential philosophy is a Western idea, originating in Europe in the 18th and 19th centuries. Buddhism is much older, said to have originated in the fifth century B.C.E. Despite their disparate origins and development, there are several striking similarities.

Heidegger, a famous existential writer, wrote a book translated as "mindfulness." He talks about being, living in the moment, throughout his writing. Buddhism, as well as other Eastern philosophies (Taoism, for instance) also focus on the importance of immersion in the moment. Mindfulness is essential to both philosophies. Mindfulness means living in the moment with full awareness.

Though this is a more integral part of existential thought (the fear of death and the need to face it permeates existentialism), Buddhism also focuses on meditating on one's death. Being aware of death is central to Tibetan Buddhism, which spurred the famous "Tibetan Book of the Dead," and more recently, "Tibetan Book of Living and Dying." Yoga has a pose called, "Savasana." Though yoga is not a Buddhist concept, nevertheless it demonstrates the fact that Eastern thought (in this case Hindu) has come to similar conclusions as western existentialism.

In India, an Upanishad called "Kathopnishad" is the legendary story of a little boy, Nachiketa – the son of Sage Vajasravasa, who meets Yama (the Indian deity of death). Their conversation evolves to a discussion of the nature of man, knowledge, Atman (Soul, Self) and Moksha (liberation).

Death is central to existentialism, Buddhism and Upanishads. The fear, dread, angst is basic to existentialists because no reason or logic can penetrate the mystery of death. Buddha left his palace when he encountered a dead man. He was not aware of death. He saw the entire futility of life in the face of death.

But the difference between western existentialists and Buddhism is that Buddha faced death deep into meditation and experienced that which is deathless, whereas existentialists remained in anguish and despair. Western existentialists have tried to solve the mystery through logic and reason, and have failed. Buddha transcended logic and reason, went into deeper layers of mind, where logic and reason dissolved. He experienced the eternal through meditation.

As already mentioned, India has developed two paths for transcendence of mind, the path of will and the path of surrender. Meditation is the path of will.

The West could not develop either meditation or spirit of surrender to God and emphasized only on rational and logical thinking.

The age of reason or Enlightenment saw rise of scientific thinking and denial of God.

Friedrich Nietzsche's famous statement was "God is dead, therefore man is free."

If God is the creator, the whole dignity of consciousness, of freedom, of love is taken away from man.

By proposing God as the creator, all responsibility and freedom is taken away from man. The whole of existence functions just at the whim of a God, the creator.

In India God was never proposed as a creator. A creator is different from its creation, just as a potter is different from the pottery that he creates.

In India God was both the creator and creation. It is non-dual or "Advaita." This is beyond the understanding of a western logician, rational thinker and existentialist.

Nietzsche's statement is based on rationality, logic and intellect. It is not based on meditation or prayer.

If there is no God and man is free, that will simply mean that man is now capable of doing anything, good or bad; there is nobody to judge him, nobody to forgive him. This freedom will be simply licentiousness.

There are other implications. If you remove God then you leave man utterly empty. How is he going to avoid freedom being reduced to licentiousness?

Friedrich Nietzsche was not aware of the Indian spirituality of meditation or prayer.

Man is free, but his freedom can only be a joy and a blessing to him if he is rooted in spirituality through meditation or prayer.

Removing God has been the greatest danger to human freedom.

Man lost meaning and significance, creativity, receptivity to find his eternal existence. That was the anguish and despair created in the west by existentialists.

There are religions without a God. Zen also does not have any God, that's its beauty.

But it has a tremendous science to transform consciousness, to bring so much awareness that you cannot commit evil.

It is not a commandment from outside; it comes from your innermost being.

Once you know your center of being, once you know you are one with the cosmos – and the cosmos has never been created, it has been there always and always, and will be there always and always, from eternity to eternity – once you know your luminous being, your hidden Gautama Buddha, it is impossible to do anything wrong; it is impossible to do anything evil; it is impossible to do any sin.

Friedrich Nietzsche in his last phase of life became almost insane. He was hospitalized, kept in a mad asylum. Such a great giant, what happened to him? He had concluded: "God is dead," but it is a negative conclusion. He became empty but his freedom was meaningless. There was no joy in it because it was only freedom from God, but for what? Freedom has two sides: from and for. The other side was missing. That drove him insane.

Emptiness always drives people insane. You need some grounding, you need some centering, and you need some relationship with existence. God being dead, all your relationship with existence is finished. God being dead, you are left alone without roots. A tree cannot live without roots, nor can you.

God was non-existential, but it was a good consolation. It used to fill people's interior.

God has been a great consolation to people in their fear, in their dread, in their awareness of old age and death, and beyond – the unknown darkness.

So Nietzsche was not insane in the last phase of his life, it was the inevitable conclusion of his negative approach. An intellect can only be negative; it can argue and criticize and be sarcastic, but it cannot give you any nourishment. From no negative standpoint can you get any nourishment. So he lost his God, and he lost his consolation. He became free just to be mad.

And it is not only Friedrich Nietzsche, so it cannot be said that it was just an accident. Many intellectual giants find themselves in mad asylums or commit suicide, because nobody can live in a negative darkness. One needs light and a positive, affirmative experience of truth. Nietzsche demolished the light and created a vacuum within him and in others who followed him.

If you feel deep down a vacuum, utter emptiness with no meaning, it is because of Friedrich Nietzsche. A whole philosophy of existentialism has grown in the West: Nietzsche is the founder of this very negative approach to life.

Soren Kierkegaard, Jean-Paul Sartre, Marcel, Jaspers, and Martin Heidegger – all the great giants of the first half of the 20th century – were talking only about meaninglessness, anguish, suffering, anxiety, dread, fear, angst. And this philosophy has been called in the West existentialism. It is not, as a matter of fact. It is simply non-existentialism. It destroys everything that has consoled man.

Out of that vacuum existentialism is born, that's why it talks only about meaninglessness: "Life has no meaning." It talks about no significance: "Man is just an accident. Whether you are here or not does not matter at all to existence."

You are not needed; just by accident, on the margin, somehow you have popped up. God was making you a puppet, and these philosophers from Nietzsche to Jean-Paul Sartre are making you accidental.

And there is a tremendous need in man's being to be related to existence. He needs roots in existence, because only when the roots go deep into existence will he blossom into a Buddha, will he blossom into millions of flowers, and will his life not be meaningless. Then his life will be tremendously overflowing with meaning, significance, blissfulness; his life will be simply a celebration.

But the conclusion of the so-called existentialists is that you are unnecessary, that your life has no meaning, no significance. Existence is not in need of you at all!

Existence according to the so-called existentialists, who are all following Friedrich Nietzsche, the founder, is absolutely unintelligent. They have taken away God, so they think – according to logic it seems apparently true – if there is no God, existence also becomes dead, with no intelligence, with no life. God used to be the life, God used to be the consciousness. God used to be the very meaning, the very salt of our being. With God no longer there, this whole existence becomes soulless, life becomes just a by-product of matter. So when you die, everything will die, nothing will remain.

Once God is removed, a great strangeness starts happening between you and existence. There is no relationship, existence does not care, cannot care because it is not conscious anymore. It is no longer an intelligent universe; it is simply dead matter, just as you are. And the life that you know is only a by-product.

Man is the highest evolution of existence, of intelligence, and it is dependent on you. If you grow higher than the mind and its intelligence, towards no-mind and its intelligence, existence is going to celebrate: one man again has reached to the ultimate peak. One part of existence has suddenly risen to the highest possibilities of the intrinsic potential in everybody…

And a man who knows his relation, his deep relation with existence, cannot commit anything against existence, against life. It is simply impossible. He can only pour as much blissfulness, as much benediction, as much grace as you are ready to receive. But his sources are inexhaustible. When you have found your inexhaustible sources of life and its ecstasy, then it does not matter whether you have a God or not.

Marx and Freud and all sorts of people have been working hard to make man godless.

Communism has been anti – God. It could not survive.

Therefore, a universal God is required for man to have a meaningful life. Communism is based on negative philosophy.

Materialism is growing because of denial of God. Life is becoming meaningless through denial of God. Greed and fear are causing negativity throughout this planet. To hide his misery man is trying to explore more and more sources of entertainment. But underneath these creature comforts and pleasures the fear haunts, the fear of death.

A personal God is not necessary for exploring one's interiority. Buddha denied God. Zen, which is an off – shoot of Buddhism, has no personal God. Meditative practices don't have any personal God.

But, as I said earlier, man needs support of a personal God in form in times of despair and existential crisis.

Tulsidas wrote in Ramcharit Manas that in this age of Kaliyuga, which is full of deceit and evil forces, there is no other option but to recite the name of Rama. Neem Karoli Baba also laid the same emphasis.

A personal God in form is necessary universally if man has to be saved from anguish and despair. One can call it idolatry, but it works to resolve and dissolve the state of despair.

Lord Rama and Hanuman are universal God and deity. They should not be viewed local to India. They must be accepted universally with trust instead of bringing logic and rationality.

One would have to know about Neem Karoli Baba to confirm existence of Rama and Hanuman.

There are social reformers who teach morality and ethics in the world to overcome negative forces. This is futile. One would lose his precious life in bringing about transformation in the world and fail.

Instead of reforms on the outside, what is required is a transformation within. For that transformation, devotion, prayer and surrender with trust and feeling is required. Logic must be abandoned for devotion and prayer.

Rama and Hanuman as Universal God

As I have described earlier, I had no faith in a personal God, never went to a temple, and never offered prayers. I was a meditator. I was a disciple of Osho. Osho laid the foundation of meditation like Buddha and Zen. He did not promote a personal God in form although he spoke a great deal on various saints like Meera, Nanak who were devotees.

But because my life was a tragic life I suffered a great deal physically, mentally and financially.

One day, I stumbled upon Neem Karoli Baba, came to know about him from the books of his devotees.

Baba attracted me immensely. The reason was that he was of the view that only when our mundane problems are resolved or dissolved our trust in God would grow.

I was gripped with mundane problems of my life. Meditation did not help me to silence my worries. I could listen to Osho's discourses, meditated, attended meditation camps but all in vain in times of crisis.

Frustrations grew in me. Logic and reason did not solve the issues.

I could see the point in Neem Karoli Baba. He did not deliver discourses, never preached but helped millions to resolve or dissolve mundane problems. Those, who came in contact with him, were immediately transformed without any spiritual practices and became devotees. They consisted of people both from the west and the east. He re-established trust in Rama and Hanuman.

Hanuman is a devotee of Rama. Hanuman is known as Sankat Mochan, which means one who takes the troubles away.

Hanuman is one character in the entire episode of Ramayana without whom nothing would move.

Rama was in trouble. His wife Sita had been taken away by Ravana in disguise. Rama did not know the whereabouts of Sita. He was living in exile in forest. Hanuman came in contact with him. Hanuman planned a strategy. He was in the service of Sugriva, who was also living in exile because his elder brother Bali had thrown him out of his kingdom and captured Sugriva's wife. Hanuman brought Rama in contact with Sugriva and helped both to come out of Sankat.

Sita was also in trouble in Lanka. Hanuman crossed the ocean, went to Lanka and met Ma Sita. He brought confidence into her.

Vibhishan, who was younger brother of Ravana, was in trouble. Hanuman brought him in contact with Rama. After the death of Ravana, Vibhishan became the king of Lanka.

There are many situations where Hanuman removed the troubles.

He was blessed by Rama and Ma Sita for immortality. He is a living deity on this planet.

A TV serial in India was produced on Ramayana by Rama Nand Sagar in the eighties. The serial has 78 episodes. An APP is available on the Playstore called Ramayana. This can be downloaded on the mobile application. The serial has English sub-titles. I highly recommend a western seeker to view this serial to know about Rama and Hanuman.

Without Neem Karoli Baba the episode of Ramayana would look like a fiction or a story. Neem Karoli Baba through his divine plays proved that he could do miracles, change destinies and bring trust amongst his devotees. He said, "I do not make disciples, only devotees."

Baba infused trust in me for Rama and Hanuman. I started praying. This generated confidence in me.

Neem Karoli Baba encouraged the constant repetition of "Rama" in order to become closer to God, saying, "By taking the name of Rama, everything is accomplished."

Therefore, I advocate a universal God in form. That God is Rama and Hanuman is the deity. Hanuman is a devotee of Rama, who performs selfless service.

Neem Karoli Baba laid the ground for selfless service amongst his devotees.

The world has lost the concept of selfless service and has become commercial in every aspect of life. Unless this is changed, the planet would suffer.

Money should be used for welfare of human beings, not for greed and hoarding. Today machines have replaced man from the drudgery of human labor. Machine should produce and man should be able to enjoy the fruits of science. But, because of various reasons, money is cleverly being controlled by the network of banking system, creating a debt – based economy, promoting production, sale and distribution of war weapons and killing millions through economic war. Economic war is the third world war.

World needs to learn from Neem Karoli Baba and Hanuman about selfless service.

Larry Brilliant, a devotee of Baba has done a great service through eradication of deadly disease Small Pox from this planet. This is an example of service to this planet.

East and West must join hands together in establishing a new world order by promoting devotion and prayer, and trust in Rama and Hanuman as a universal God and deity.

6
Western and Eastern Approaches to Resolve Human Anxiety, Worry and Misery

This book is about Neem Karoli Baba.

India is a land full of saints, sages, gurus and masters since ancient times.

Saints, sages, gurus and masters are different categories of fully conscious beings to help man to grow into the divinity.

In my view, divinity is there when one is in a state of non-misery. Misery can be physical, spiritual and material. (Physical includes mental). A state of non-misery is when one is full of energy – physical, mental and spiritual. This energy is called Love or God.

Negativity, anxiety and worry eat away our energy and one lives as if lifeless, without love.

I never met Neem Karoli Baba, never went to his Ashram. There are no preachings, no books from him except by his devotees who have compiled experiences of various visitors/devotees/householders visiting him. But even without meeting him I could experience his divine spiritual energy and love for life.

I was a disciple of a master "Osho." Osho had initiated me in neo-Sannyas about 40 years ago. He was a master par excellence, one of the greatest enlightened masters who ever walked on this planet.

I meditated in his presence, heard his thought-provoking discourses and ran a meditation centre for long many years. He gave the name of my meditation centre "Satpriti" which meant true love. Sitting in his presence was a great divine experience; it was an energy – field, which he called Buddha-field. I gained considerable insight reading Osho. He had a wonderful memory, his learning was unparalleled; his discourses could take one to exalted states. I could never imagine anybody could reach such heights.

Why was then I attracted to Neem Karoli Baba?

I was in a state of misery both in my personal and professional life. I missed love everywhere.

Meditation was unable to produce that love.

Osho was not accessible to individuals. He did not listen to the personal problems of his disciples. He only delivered discourses before gatherings of his disciples. He chose the questions himself that he thought were worth – answering. During the evenings, he gave "Energy Darshan." This continued till 1981. Only westerners were allowed to ask about personal problems. He answered their concerns, gave advice and asked them to participate in some group therapies. His replies are compiled in his books known as "Darshan Diaries." Group therapies were psychotherapy groups intended to cathart repressed feelings like sex, anger etc. His ashram made considerable money from these psychotherapy group therapies. These were not meant for Indians. His Ashram was managed mostly by westerners supported by some Indian female disciples. The entire outlook was westernized. After he left his mortal frame, the Pune Ashram has become a resort; It has become expensive and beyond the reach of not so well-to-do Indians.

I did not find any solution to my worries. Osho had devised many meditation techniques. His emphasis was to cathart repressed feelings.

Meditation did bring silent energy but could not last when worries surrounded mind. Osho was capable of arguing for and against any subject. This made many confused. That was his strategy. He did not want any cult to be born around him. By contradicting his own statements, he would throw the burden on the listener to choose what was right for him. His strategy was to demolish all the old and rotten religions from the planet so that a new man could be born free from any prejudices. Before he left his body, he declared to his disciples "I leave you my dream." He could not fulfill his dream during his lifetime.

Dreams are unreal events. Dreams cannot be fulfilled. Osho had dreamt of something, and wanted others to fulfill it. This is a contradiction in terms. I don't see any possibility of his dream ever being fulfilled by his disciples. Disciples can only ritualistically meditate as per various techniques devised by Osho but cannot fulfill his dream of a new man "Zorba, the Buddha."

I was getting disenchanted because of my personal worries.

I became physically sick, was diagnosed suffering from colon cancer, and remained bedridden and worried mentally.

At this juncture, Neem Karoli Baba came into my life.

The more I read about him, the more I was thrilled. He was love personified.

Here was a man who was more interested in solving mundane problems.

There have been incarnations (avatar) in various ages in India. All the incarnations are of Lord Vishnu taking birth on this planet to empower the good and fight against the evil.

In Hinduism dashavatara (दशावतार) refers to the ten primary avatars of Vishnu, the Hindu god of preservation. These are: Matsya, Kurma, Varaha, Narasimha, Vamana, Parashurama, Rama, Krishna, Buddha, and Kalki. Out of these, Matsya, Kurma, Varaha and Narasimha avatars happened in Satyuga. Vamana, Parashurama and Rama avatars happened in Treta Yuga. Krishna happened in Dwapar Yuga. Buddha, the ninth avatar happened in this age of Kaliyuga. Kalki avatar is the last avatar yet to happen in Kaliyuga.

Neem Karoli Baba is not an avatar of Vishnu. He is an avatar or incarnation of Lord Hanuman.

It is known that Lord Hanuman is the 11th rudra avatar of Lord Shiva and since Lord Shiva is known as the destructor of evil, Lord Hanuman is known as the destructor of troubles (Sankat Mochan)… Hence, Lord Hanuman is known as an incarnation of Lord Shiva or Rudra Avatar.

Neem Karoli Baba is also Sankat Mochan.

The difference between a master and incarnation should be understood. A master preaches the preachings, which are subsequently collected in the form of scriptures. Holy Bible, Holy Quran, Dhammapada, Tao-Te Ching etc are scriptures. These are collections of words from different masters.

I was a disciple of a master "Osho." He delivered discourses, which are published in over 650 books in Hindi and English. Due to the technological advancement, his spoken words are now available in audio/video format. There is no need for any interpreter, which was needed in ancient days by the disciples of various masters, be it Jesus or Mohammed or others.

But incarnations are different from masters. As far as I know, there is no concept of incarnation in the western world. Even master and disciple relations as it exists in India, do not exist anywhere else, to the best of my knowledge.

A master preaches. He helps his disciples to understand nature and God. He develops techniques to overcome misery and worries.

But as far as incarnations are concerned, there are no recorded preachings or scriptures.

The life of incarnations is called a divine play or "Lila." These divine plays have been written in the form of epics by the devotees. Through these epics the lives of incarnations are known.

When the descriptions of the divine plays become ancient, they are called "Puranas." The word 'Purana' literally means "ancient, old," and it is a vast genre of Indian literature about a wide range of topics, particularly myths, legends and other traditional lore. Different Puranas describe a number of stories about Brahma, Vishnu and Shiva, the trinity of Gods of Hindus.

Rama is the seventh avatar of Vishnu. The epic "Ramayana" by Valmiki describes the life of Rama in Sanskrit. Later Tulsidas wrote "Ramcharitmanas" in vernacular language, which is very popular in north India.

With the passage of time, people believe the epics as a story, a fiction or a play. Their authenticity is lost in the oblivion. These become myths.

Neem Karoli Baba broke these myths through his incarnation in human form. Devotees who witnessed Baba's divine plays are alive; their recorded versions have still not become "Puranas" or myth. Baba revived the legend of Rama and Hanuman.

The purpose for revival of the divine spirit is to bring confidence in human beings about existence of higher beings to protect human beings and the planet from evil spirits. Existence loves His creation.

The difference between Rama and Hanuman should also be clearly understood. Both are incarnations. But Rama is an incarnation of Lord Vishnu, one of the trinity of Gods in Hinduism and Hanuman is a partial incarnation of Lord Shiva, another trinity God.

As explained in previous chapters, Gods in Hinduism are the attributes of the formless God called "Brahma." Vishnu is an attribute, Shiva is also an attribute. Vishnu is the sustainer of life, Shiva is the destroyer. Both work hand-in-glove. Birth and death are two sides of the same coin.

Gods incarnate in human form to rid this planet of global issues. In "Treta Yuga" and "Dwapar Yuga," God incarnated as Rama and Krishna to rid the planet of evil spirits. But in "Kaliyuga" God has still not incarnated (?) so far. It is said that the incarnation would happen when Vishnu is born as "Kalki" avatar.

Hanuman is a partial incarnation of Lord Shiva. He is a true devotee of Lord Rama. A devotee is a stepping – stone to take one to God.

Both Rama and Hanuman work hand – in – glove. Rama as an incarnation of Lord Vishnu establishes order to sustain life on this planet, and Hanuman helps Rama by helping those who are in trouble and unable to live because of evil forces.

Hanuman solves individual's problems too. Those who worship Rama are automatically helped by Hanuman. Hanuman does not solve global issues. People, who suffer individually due to global issues, are protected by Hanuman. Wars whether fought by weapons or on economic front are global issues which are causing sufferings to individuals. Hanuman protects those devotees who are in "Sankat" or misery due to various issues. He does not solve global issues. In Treta Yuga, it was Rama who killed Ravana. Hanuman helped Rama in his mission to kill evil forces as a devotee. Hanuman was a perfect devotee and Rama loved him very much. Without Hanuman, it would have been difficult for Rama to destroy the evil forces. Hanuman is a deity, Rama is a God.

Neem Karoli Baba also helped millions of individuals who suffered because of myriad of mundane issues. Many persons thought that Baba should, instead of bothering to solve worldly problems of the individuals, only engage himself in various spiritual practices. But for Baba mundane problems were more important. By solving mundane issues, Baba could infuse trust in Rama and God even amongst atheists and non-believers.

Spirituality is the science to transcend human misery, worry, and anxiety through the support of divine energies and love.

Western Psychological Techniques to Resolve Mental Worries

Worry, anxiety and misery have been eating away human energy on this planet particularly after the growth of science and technology. Love has become non-existent. Western countries are working hard to solve human worries and anxiety through psychotherapy, hypnotherapy and myriad of other techniques.

Anxiety and worry amongst humans is increasing and giving rise to various psychosomatic disorders.

Animal, plants, birds don't suffer from misery the same way as man suffers. It is a common sight to see the high energy amongst forest beasts compared to man. Why does it happen?

This is due to evolution of mind or consciousness amongst humans. Man needs love.

Love is of two kinds: one is instinctive, the other is spiritual.

A mother loves a child through instincts. That is the love given by nature. The love between wife and husband is also not spiritual. It is mixed with sex.

Mental health professionals are growing in the world. Many of these methods are individual based on interaction of the professional with the client. Some are conducted in groups including families. Psychotherapists, mental health professionals such as psychiatrists, psychologists, clinical social workers, marriage and family therapists, or professional counselors are technique oriented; there is no base of love.

Hypnotherapy is undertaken while a subject is in a state of hypnosis. Hypnotherapy is often applied in order to modify a subject's behavior, emotional content, and attitudes, as well as a wide range of conditions including dysfunctional habits, anxiety, stress-related illness, pain management, and personal development. Hypnotherapy is also technique – oriented without a base of love.

Man is today gripped more with psychological disorders compared to physical diseases. Most of the physical illnesses arise out of worry and anxiety in the mind. In my view, it is basically lack of love that is causing all the disorders.

Richard Alpert, a clinical psychologist in America, stumbled upon Neem Karoli Baba. He was experimenting with hallucinogenic drugs such as psilocybin, LSD-25, and other psychedelic chemicals to achieve altered state of consciousness. He often participated in group LSD sessions, looking for a permanent route to higher consciousness. Psychologists thought that with the support of these drugs a man could reach exalted states and could transcend mundane issues, which were eating away the energy.

In 1967, Alpert traveled to India where he met and traveled with the American spiritual seeker Bhagavan Das, and ultimately met the man who would become his guru, Neem Karoli Baba at Kainchi ashram, whom Alpert called "Maharajji." It was Maharajji who gave Alpert the name "Ram Dass," which means "servant of Rama," referring to the incarnation of God as Ram or Lord Rama.

In 1967, when he first came to India, he brought with him a supply of LSD, hoping to find someone who might understand more about these substances. When he met Maharajji, after some days he thought that Maharajij would be a perfect person to ask.

Even before Ram Dass could have the courage to ask, Maharajji himself said,"Where is the medicine?" Ram Dass brought the bottle of LSD from his car and emptied the vial of pills into his hand.

Maharajji held out his hand for the LSD. Ram Dass put one pill in his palm. Each of the pills was about 300 micrograms of very pure LSD – a solid dose for an adult. Maharajji asked for more and threw all the pills into his mouth. Ram Dass was shocked. He was eager to see what happened.

Maharajji allowed him to stay for an hourand nothing happened. He just laughed at Ram Dass.

A few years later, when Ram Dass returned to India, he gave 4 pills each of 300 micrograms. Maharajji swallowed all the pills one by one in his mouth. At the end of an hour nothing happened. He asked, "Have you got anything stronger?" Ram Dass did not have anything more.

Maharajij said; "These medicines were used by Yogis but the knowledge has been lost. They were used with fasting. Nobody knows now. To take them with no effect, your mind must be firmly fixed on God. Many saints would not take this."

When Ram Dass asked him whether he should take LSD again, he said," It should not be taken in a hot climate. If you are in a place that is cool and peaceful, and you are alone and your mind is turned towards God, then you may take the yogi medicine."

"LSD is good for the world but is not spiritual. "LSD is not true Samadhi," Baba said.

Ram Dass received love from Maharajji. He wrote a book "Miracle of Love."

What is important is that psychotherapy in the west should be based on love. Love is the greatest healer. Sigmund Freud, who is the founder of psychoanalysis, was an atheist. Since the development of science, the west has lost track with spirituality and love. India is no exception. The influence of western culture through the use of scientific gadgets has changed the culture in large cities. But faith in spirituality still prevails in villages and small towns. Villagers still love and have a concern for the other.

Hippie Culture

During the mid-sixties, a youth movement started in America, which spread to other countries of the world. A July 1968 Time magazine study on hippie philosophy credited the foundation of the hippie movement with historical precedent as far back as the Sadhus of India, the spiritual seekers who had renounced the world by taking "Sannyas." Hippie culture spread worldwide through a fusion of rock music, folkblues, and psychedelic rock. On October 6, 1966, the state of California declared LSD a controlled substance, which made the drug illegal.

Contrary to this, those who took LSD said, " They were not guilty of using illegal substances… We were celebrating transcendental consciousness, the beauty of the universe, the beauty of being."

Harvard University professors Timothy Leary, Ralph Metzner and Richard Alpert (Ram Dass) advocated psychotropic drugs for psychotherapy, self-exploration, religious and spiritual use. Regarding LSD, Leary said, "Expand your consciousness and find ecstasy and revelation within"

Hippies revolted against established traditions. Most of the Americans who came to Baba were hippies. They came to India in search of spirituality. Most of them travelled to Varanasi.

From 1968 to1971, I was at Varanasi teaching electronics engineering at the Banaras Hindu University. I saw the hippie culture in Varanasi. Varanasi is said to be a holy place where Lord Shiva resides. Lord Shiva is the oldest Hippie. He uses intoxicants of all sorts for his Yoga. That was the reason for western hippies to travel to Varanasi.

Another place where hippies would travel was Kathmandu in Nepal. The famous Pashupati Nath temple of Lord Shiva is located in Kathmandu.

Intoxicants were used in India for spiritual practices and not for worldly pleasures. Hippies and psychoanalysts were not aware anything about Indian spirituality and were doing experiments in dark using their mind.

The same mistake was done by Sigmund Freud, who was trying to use analytical methods to treat psychopathology cases without any spiritual support of love.

According to Freud's model of the psyche, the id is the primitive and instinctual part of the mind that contains sexual and aggressive drives and hidden memories, the super-ego operates as a moral conscience, and the ego is the realistic part that mediates between the desires of the id and the super-ego.

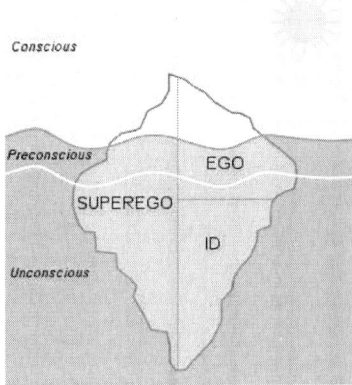

Freud's model of Mind

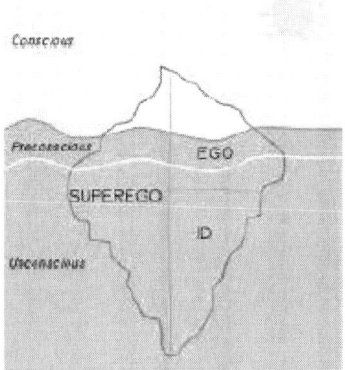

Id, Superego and Ego

The id, ego and super-ego are purely psychological concepts and do not correspond to (somatic) structures of the brain such as the kind dealt with by neuroscience.

The id is the disorganized part of the personality structure that contains a human's basic, instinctual drives. Id is the only component of personality that is present from birth. It is the source of our bodily needs, wants, desires, and impulses, particularly our sexual and aggressive drives. The id contains the libido, which is the primary source of instinctual force that is unresponsive to the demands of reality. The id acts according to the "pleasure principle"—the psychic force that motivates the tendency to seek immediate gratification of any impulse—defined as seeking to avoid pain or displeasure aroused by increases in instinctual tension. According to Freud, the id is unconscious by definition.

The ego acts according to the reality principle.

The super-ego reflects the internalization of cultural rules, mainly taught by parents applying their guidance and influence.

Freud's analysis of dreams as wish-fulfillments provided him with models for the clinical analysis of symptom formation and the underlying mechanisms of repression. He thought sex was the repressed desire in the unconscious, which caused various mental disorders. He experimented with dreams of his clients to establish sexual repression.

Sex, anger etc are instincts given to humans in the unconscious mind for survival.

Love is transformation of sex. In India, "Tantric" experiments were done for transcendence of sex into love.

Freud maintained that religion – once necessary to restrain man's violent nature in the early stages of civilization – in modern times, can be set aside in favor of reason and science.

Freud was an atheist and was influenced by Nietzsche.

Both Freud and existentialists denied God.

Freud's method was analytical, devoid of raising human energy with the support of a divine energy. Therefore, Psychoanalysis has failed. Unless human energy can be made to grow through love, it cannot raise the vitality. India has always been in support of raising consciousness through meditation or prayer and love. Indian methods are based on trust; western methods are based on doubt, reason and logic.

I would like to explain the map of the mind both according to the modern psychology, and also according to the eastern yoga of Patanjali.

This would clarify why man is in misery and how spirituality can take a man into a state of non-misery.

The figure below is a map showing various layers of the mind. It cannot be dissected by medical science. But it fits well to explain the concept of human mind.

An iceberg is shown below floating in an ocean. This iceberg can be taken to represent the human mind.

That part of the iceberg that is seen above the water is called the conscious mind. This is that portion of mind that is used for reasoning, logic and decision – making. Conscious mind is only the tip of the iceberg as shown in the picture. It is about 10% of the total mind. 90% of the mind remains under water and is called subconscious and the unconscious mind.

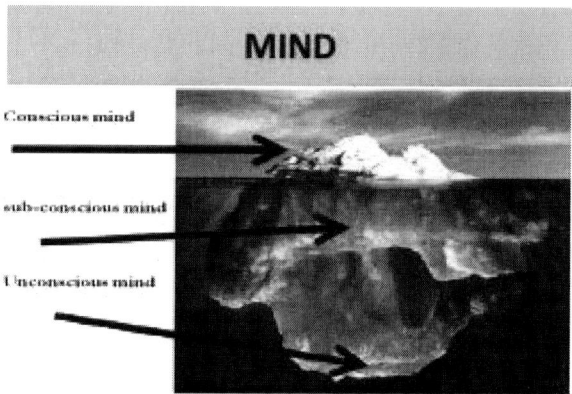

Conscious mind works during the waking hours. Sub-conscious mind works during sleep for dreaming. Unconscious mind is buried still deeper in the dark and works during dreamless sleep.

Hindus have explained evolution of life on this planet in terms of "Jagrati" (waking), Swapnil" (Dreaming) and "Sushupti" (Deep Sleep) states of the mind. A rock is in the "Sushupti" or deep sleep state of the consciousness. Life has still not evolved; it is still in the form of mineral rocks. All the minerals in our body are evidence of our evolution from the rocks. Sodium, Potassium, Calcium, Iron, Manganese etc are minerals in our body needed for sustenance of life. Any disbalance causes physical and mental disorder.

Life evolves from rocks into plants, birds and animals. In terms of evolution of consciousness, they are said to be in the "Swapnil" or dream state.

With humans the consciousness evolved further in the waking state, which is represented by the top of the iceberg above water. Man has become partially conscious. He can reason out, analyze and take decisions. Development of science, mathematics is due to this top of the iceberg.

But man has denied growth of the remaining layers of the mind and has used so far only the 10% of the conscious mind, which Freud calls ego. This is the cause of misery on this planet. This conscious mind wills and is the self or ego according to Hinduism. Man thinks and through thinking will is created. Man thinks that he can will anything through reason, logic and science and denies everything else. But man forgets that many essential activities for survival do not happen by will; they are involuntary. For example, breathing, blood circulation, digestion, sleep and even sex cannot be willed, these are not under the conscious control of man. These are unconscious and instinctive.

Hindus have called all those activities divine that happen involuntarily without man's will. Hindus have worshipped sleep and called it "Nidra Devi," sex as "Kamadeva" because these are not caused by will.

If the consciousness grows, man can transcend nature. He no longer remains slave to the nature's instincts that are hidden in the unconscious layers of the mind. He can transcend sex, anger; fear greed etc, which are instinctive and part of the unconscious mind. Neem Karoli Baba had transcended nature. Nature was under his control.

So long as man is under the control of nature's instincts, he functions unconsciously, evil spirits dominate. These are destructive energies, if not used consciously. Life suffers on this planet when unconsciousness grows. According to Hindus, when evil dominates, God incarnates in human form for establishing order on this planet. This planet is special because life has evolved on it. The purpose of life is to grow consciousness so that man can rise to Godliness. It has taken billions of years for life to evolve on this planet. God is interested that life should come to full circle through full evolution of consciousness.

The fall of Adam and Eve from the Garden of Eden is the story of man being thrown out of God. Man has been thrown so that he can learn, grow and rise again to go back to the Garden of Eden.

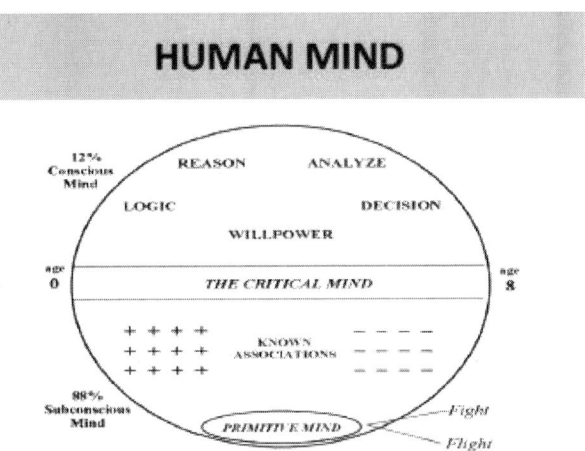

The above picture is a map of the mind showing its different layers.

When a child is born, he has a primitive mind. It is the unconscious layer of the mind. There are two instincts in the primitive mind. It is called fight/flight mechanism. The child has two fears, the fear of falling and the fear of noise.

Subsequently, the child learns by association and identification.

From age zero to approximately age eight, the child develops a library of these associations and identifications. He/she learns that some of these are good (positive) and some of these are bad (negative). These positive and negative associations form what is referred to as our "life script." This life script is formed from what we know. The child does not yet know "good" from "bad" or "right" from "wrong." He/she is only aware of the associations and identifications. During this period, subconscious mind evolves.

Whatever is taught by the parents and the society gets imprinted into the subconscious layers of the mind. This part of the mind is a storehouse of all learning. Priests and society have used this layer of mind to indoctrinate the child about their religions at an early age. This learning becomes a script giving rise to religious fanaticism. All educational systems tap the subconscious mind for teaching and learning.

Between the ages of eight and twelve (approximately), we start to develop logic and reason. We are capable of making decisions and developing will power. This becomes our conscious mind, which represents 12% of our total mind power. The subconscious mind is made up of the remaining 88% of our total mind power. According to Hindus, the unconscious mind is a store – house of all the past life memories, cellular memories from the beginning of the evolution for survival of the body.

Fight/Flight Reaction (Anxiety and Depression)

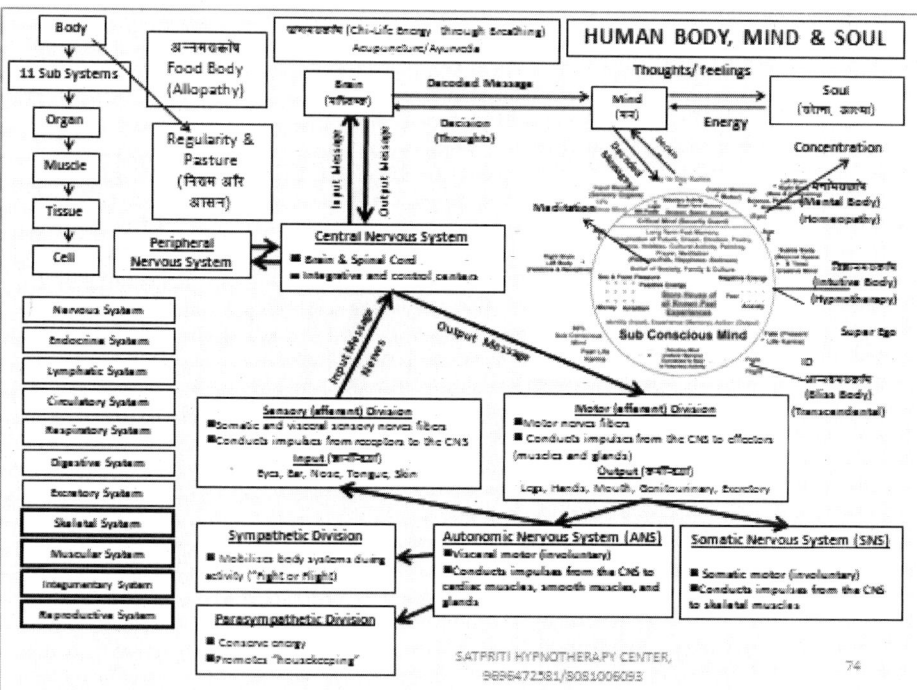

Above picture shows the map of body system and the mind.

The human body consists of 11 subsystems. These are:

Nervous system, Endocrine System, Lymphatic System, Circulatory System, Digestive System, Respiratory System, Skeletal System, Muscular System, Integumentary system (Skin) and reproductive system.

The picture above shows how inputs are received by the body and mind, and then a decision to act is taken by the mind, brain, the nervous system and the organs.

Input from the environment is sensed by the sensory organs. There are five sensory organs. Hindus call it "Gyanendriya." These are: skin, eyes, ears, nose, and tongue. The inputs from these sensory organs are delivered to the nervous System. Nervous system delivers it to the brain; brain to the mind for a decision. Brain is like hardware of a computer and mind is the software.

Fight/Flight is nature's inbuilt mechanism to safeguard life from dangers. It is a primitive and involuntary reaction that is triggered by a perceived sense of danger or during a state of anxiety, in order to defend oneself or to escape from danger. This triggering is done through mind, brain, nervous system and work-organs, which Hindus call "Karmendriyas." These five organs of action are: Pada (feet) – for locomotion. Pani (hands) – for dexterity, Payu (rectum) – for excretion, Upastha (genitals) – for reproduction, Vak (mouth) – for speech.

Primitive man survived by developing two basic instincts. These instincts are called Fight and Flight mechanisms. Man (and some creatures) had developed greater strength and aggression (fight), while others developed speed, agility and sensitivity toward their surroundings using their sense of smell, hearing and sight (flight). Creatures that were able to develop both fight and flight abilities survived to evolve, others became extinct.

Autonomic Nervous System

Autonomic Nervous System is that part of the nervous system that works to activate Fight/Flight mechanism.

There are two divisions of the autonomic nervous system:

Sympathetic: Activated during the fight/flight mechanism.

Parasympathetic: A self – regulating stabilizing system that brings us back to a state of balance.

During sympathetic arousal, physiological changes occur, preparing the body for fight/flight. After the danger has passed, the parasympathetic system takes over to create a homeostasis (balance).

Depression

Originally, man functioned completely on basic instincts. He did not have inhibitions. Modesty, privacy and sexual taboos were some of the earlier inhibitions to develop.

As man evolved, he came to the realization that he did not have to act on every impulse that confronted him. He then started to develop conscious control.

Fight/flight mechanism given to man and animals by nature is to safeguard against physical dangers.

Anger and fear were two basic components of instinctive energy for fight/flight mechanism.

With the progress of civilization man was able to safeguard the body by building cities, dwellings and remaining safely away from the beasts.

But the danger arose between man and man. Greed and hatred are also components of anger and fear. With the growth of civilization, anger became anxiety, and fear became depression. Because anxiety and fear are repressed by man and not expressed, it has led to various psychosomatic disorders.

When the **fight mechanism started to become anxiety,** man started to feel it in his body. The modern way of looking at this is reaction versus action. The flight mechanism also developed a modern way of coping. This can be seen as repression versus depression. The modern **flight mechanism is depression.**

Auto Immune Disorders due to Anxiety and Depression

Several physical disorders develop on account of involuntary triggering mechanism of the autonomic nervous system due to anxiety and depression.

The endocrine and lymphatic system are affected which disturb hormones in the body and the defense mechanism for protection from the environment.

In cases of **immune system** over activity, the body attacks and damages its own tissues (autoimmune diseases). Immune deficiency diseases **decrease** the body's ability to fight invaders, causing vulnerability to **infections**. Asthma, Arthritis, Graves' disease, Lupus, Type 1 diabetes. Multiple sclerosis (MS), Rheumatoid arthritis are a few common auto – immune diseases.

I have tried to explain the reason for anxiety and depression using the western psychological model of mind.

The anxiety and depression are negative energies. Unless love is introduced to transform these negative energies, psychotherapy would not help.

Patanjali's Yoga Sutras

The body systems were also the subject of study by Maharshi Patanjali of India.

Maharshi Patanjali was a seer who compiled the entire system of Raja Yoga or Hatha Yoga.

Patanjali wrote Yoga Sutras or "Yoga aphorisms."

Yoga in Indian traditions is more than physical exercise; it has a meditative and spiritual core, one of the six major orthodox schools of Hinduism is also called Yoga, which has its own epistemology and metaphysics, and is closely related to Hindu Samkhya philosophy.

According to Patanjali, "Yoga is the cessation of the mind."

"Yogaś citta-vritti-nirodhaḥ" refers to stilling the mind in order to experience Ultimate Reality and move toward Self-realization.

As I have said earlier, mind is misery. Cessation of fluctuations of mind (Vrittis of Chitta) takes one into the state of non-misery or Anand.

Patañjali divided his *Yoga Sutras* into four chapters or books (Sanskrit *pada*), containing in all 196 aphorisms, divided as follows: **Samadhi Pada** (51 sutras). **Sadhana Pada** (55 sutras). Vibhuti **Pada** (56 sutras) **Kaivalya Pada** (34 sutras).

Out of the above four chapters, the chapter 3 called Vibhuti Pada (56 sutras) discusses about body systems, practice of Dhāraṇā, Dhyana and Samādhi referred to as Samyama, and is considered a tool of achieving various perfections, or Siddhis.

Vibhuti is the Sanskrit word for "power" or "manifestation."

'Supra-normal powers' (Sanskrit: Siddhi) are acquired by the practice of yoga. The text, however, warns that these powers can become an obstacle to the yogi who seeks liberation.

Lord Hanuman is gifted by all the Siddhi's or powers. Neem Karoli Baba is also gifted with all the Siddhi's. But they have not misused these powers. These miraculous powers were used for service to the Lord. Hanuman as a perfect devotee of Rama used Siddhis for helping Rama and others for a divine purpose. Neem Karoli Baba like Hanuman also used miracles through various Siddhi's in the service of mankind.

To understand about Siddhis we would have to understand the concept of body and mind as enunciated by Patanjali in Vibhuti Pada of Yoga Sutras.

Five Body Systems, Five Mahabhutas and Seven Chakras according to Patanjali's Yoga Sutra in Vibhuti Pada

Patanjali divides human personality into five seeds, five bodies. We don't have only one body but there are layers and layers of bodies one behind the other.

The first body is called **"Annamaya Kosh,"** the food body. This body is made of earth and other basic elements and is nourished by food. Yoga demands purity of food for entering the second body. The right amount of food and the right quality of food has to be practised, the first body is gross.

The second body is called **"Pranámaya Kosh," energy body, and electric body.** The second body is more subtle than the first. People who move from the first body to the second body become fields of energy, attractive, magnetic, and hypnotic. If you go near them you will feel vitalized, charged. If you go near a man who lives only in the first body, you will be depleted, he will suck you.

The second body surrounds you like an aura of energy. In Soviet Russia, they have discovered that photographs can be taken of the energy body. They call it bio – plasma, it means Prana. This energy is called élan vital; Taoists call it "Chi."

Kirlian photography can take photograph of the Prana body. Below is shown the machine which can photograph aura energy.

BIO-WELL MACHINE

Electro-photonic imaging machine for imaging subtle body energy

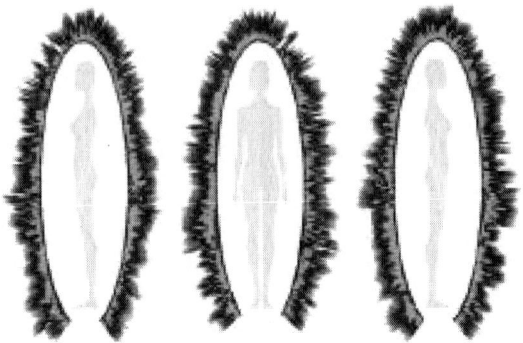

Human Aura Photograph through Kirlian photography

One discovery has revealed that before the physical body suffers some illness, the energy body suffers it six months in advance. If someone is going to have tuberculosis or cancer or any illness, the energy body starts showing indications of it six months before. No examination, no testing of the physical body shows anything, but the electric body starts showing it. So now it is possible to treat a person before he has fallen ill. Disease can be prevented in the Pranamaya Kosh.

The second body is stronger than the first body. Also second body lives longer than the first. If somebody dies, his bioplasma can be seen for almost three days. Around the Samadhi of the yogis, it can continue for much longer. That is why in India devotees go to visit Samadhi of their gurus.

Subtle body energy is affected by mental worries and anxiety. The energy level can be detected in body systems and organs six months in advance before onset of a disease on the physical body. "Pranayama" or deep breathing exercises, meditation and prayer enhance the energy and make one healthy physically, mentally and spiritually. This is the Hindu way of therapy using spiritual support, which does not exist in western psychotherapeutic methods.

ANALYSIS

Conclusions and Recommendations From Energy Field Analysis

Durga Prasad Pandey 2016-09-10

The power of the Energy Field is OPTIMAL.
The level of anxiety is OPTIMAL.
Energy balance is OPTIMAL.

Functional condition of organs and systems

System	Organ	Energy	Disbalance
Head energy			
	Eyes energy		
	Ears, nose, maxillary sinus energy		
	Jaw, Teeth energy		
	Throat, larynx, trachea energy		
	Thyroid gland energy		
	Cerebral zone (cortex) energy		
Cardiovascular system energy			
	Cardiovascular system energy		
	Heart energy		
	Cerebral zone (vessels) energy		
	Coronary vessels energy		
Respiratory system energy			
	Throat, larynx, trachea energy		
	Mammary glands (for women), Respiratory system energy		
	Thorax zone energy		
Endocrine system energy			
	Hypothalamus energy		
	Epiphysis energy		
	Hypophysis energy		
	Thyroid gland energy		
	Pancreas energy		
	Adrenals energy		
	Spleen energy		
Musculoskeletal system energy			
	Spine - cervical zone energy		

Analysis of System and Organ Energy through Kirlian photography

The third body is called **"Manomaya Kosh," the mental body.**

The third is bigger than the second, subtler than the second, and also higher than the second. Animals have the second body but not the third body. Animals are therefore so vital because mind does not attack the second body.

The word "man" comes from "Manomaya." It is the mind that comes to man.

I have already discussed about different layers of mind.

The mind grows only when we encounter a situation on our own. You bring your own energy to solve it. Prayer or devotion is a method to seek divine support.

Higher than Manomaya Kosh is **Vigyanmaya Kosha. It is the intuitive body.** It is very very spacious. It goes beyond reason. It is a seeing directly into the nature of things. It is not trying to think about it. You simply become available, receptive and reality reveals to you. You are simply waiting. This waiting is prayer and devotion. This is part of Vigyanmaya Kosh.

The fifth body is **Anandmaya Kosh, bliss body.** Even intuition is transcended.

Beyond the five bodies is our reality. Once all the five bodies are dropped, God is revealed. Hindus have called it **"Brahma."**

Corresponding to these five seeds, yoga has another doctrine about five **Bhutas, five great elements.**

Body is made of five elements: Earth, Fire, Water, Air and Ether or space.

Earth is the first element. This element simply means matter. The material is earth, the gross is the earth. The stars are made of earth i.e. matter.

The other four elements are: **Fire, Water, Air, Ether or Space.**

Earth corresponds to **Annamaya Kosha, the food body.**

Fire corresponds to the second body, the **energy body, bio plasma, chi, Pranayama Kosh;** it has the quality of fire.

Water corresponds to the third **Manomaya Kosha; the mental body.** It has the quality of water. **Mind** flows like a flux, river – like, always moving.

Air corresponds to the intuitive body, **Vigyanmaya Kosh.** Air is almost invisible, you cannot see it but you can feel it.

Ether or Akash corresponds to the **Anandmaya Kosh, the bliss body.** It has become subtlest, you can trust it that it is there.

Beyond these five bodies is the **no-self or anatta** as Buddha calls it.

These are **five Bhutas, five great elements** corresponding to **five Koshas, bodies** within us.

Then there are **seven chakras. Chakras are dynamic energy fields.** These seven chakras are as below:

Muladhar (Sex Centre – Bridge between man and Prakriti or nature), Swadhishthan (Hara-Death Centre), Manipur (Naval Centre – Reservoir of Energy), Anahata (Heart Centre), Vishuddha (Throat Centre), Agya (Third Eye Centre), Sahasrara (Bridge with the divine).

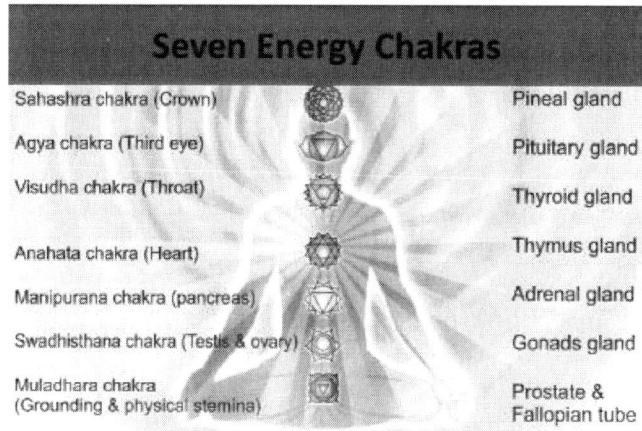

The energy fields called "Chakras" have to be awakened through yogic spiritual practices to come to a full potential.

Five bodies, five Mahabhutas and seven centers is the framework of Patanjali. A yogi works for bringing **Samyama** to become enlightened. Then one is not confined, one becomes boundless, infinite. All the imprisonments break.

By bringing **Samyama** on any matter a yogi can make it appear or disappear. A yogi can help things materialize because they come out of nothingness. Matter can become non-matter, no-matter becomes matter.

When a star dies, it becomes a black hole. Star becomes nothingness. What nature does can also be done by a yogi because nature is under his control.

Neem Karoli Baba had full control over nature. He could produce anything out of nothing. He could produce milk, ghee and petrol out of water. These are not myths. There are eye – witnesses who have recorded these miracles in their books.

Hanuman was also gifted with all the Siddhis. Tulsidas wrote in Ramcharit Manas:

"अष्ट सिद्धि नव निधि के दाता, अस बर दीन जानकी माता"

"Asht siddhi nav nidhi ke data, as bar deen janaki mata"

Meaning thereby, Ma Janaki gave a boon to Hanuman that he could bestow the eight Siddhis and nine nidhis to his devotees

Thus without undergoing the difficult spiritual practice as enunciated by Patanjali in Vibhutipada, Hanuman could bestow the Siddhis through prayer and devotion.

That was the reason why Neem Karoli Baba was not in favor of difficult spiritual practices and was always in favor of remembering Lord Rama and his devotee Hanuman.

Male-Female Principle

Life is energy, and energy is polar. The polarity means that the opposites are complementary to each other, they support each other. Life cannot exist without death; hence, death is not the enemy. It prepares the ground for life: it helps life, it provokes life, and it challenges life.

Life exists because there is death. Death gives intensity to life. Death challenges life, it provokes to live to the maximum, at the optimum, because – who knows – there may be no tomorrow. Death is always provoking you, goading you to live, and to live totally. Then death is not against life but a friend.

So is the case with all the polarities: the negative and the positive love and hate beauty and ugliness, day and night, summer and winter. And so is the case with man and woman. Man cannot be without woman, and woman cannot be without man. They are part of one dialectical process. Between these two poles there is both attraction and repulsion, because attraction and repulsion cannot be separated. Hence, you feel attracted towards woman or towards man and repulsed at the same time. A part of you wants to be with the woman, a part of you wants to be alone.

Conscious and Sub-conscious Mind		
Conscious Mind	LEFT RIGHT	Subconscious Mind
Logic		Recognition
Reason		Rhythm
Mathematics		Visual
Reading		Imagery
Writing		Creativity
Language		Dreams
Analysis		Symbols
Ego		Emotions

The conscious mind is logical, it reasons. The subconscious mind dreams, imagines. The left brain represents male, the right brain represents female. With the predominance of science, the left brain has gained supremacy and the right brain has been repressed. That is the cause of misery, anguish, anxiety.

Man has become unbalanced. Prayer can bring that balance.

The right-side brain is the seat of imagination, poetry, love, intuition. The left – side brain is the seat of reason, logic, argumentation, philosophy, science.

And unless one can attain to a balance between the sun and moon energy, one will not be able to transcend. Unless the left – side brain meets with the right-side brain and is bridged, one will not reach to Sahasrara. One has to become one to reach Sahasrara because Sahasrara is the omega point in our being. You cannot reach there as man, you cannot reach there as woman. You have to reach there just as pure consciousness – one, total, whole.

Yin-Yang Symbol

In the Hindu scripture, God is one but it manifests in nature as two. In Chinese scripture, Tao is one but it manifests as Yin and Yang, the feminine and masculine principle. It has become matter and consciousness. The whole life consists of these two principles, and behind these two principles is hidden the one. These opposites are not opposites but complimentary. We can call it Shiva and Shakti.

Ardhanarishvara

No man is only man and no woman is only woman. Man is both, woman is both; both are both. Man contains a woman within him, and so is the case with a woman: the woman contains a man within her. So it is not only a question of the outside man or outside woman, it is also an inner phenomenon, because the outer and the inner correspond.

Your inner reality is also the same as your outer reality: they correspond, they balance. Now more complexity arises because each man has a woman within him, and he has to come to terms with her. It is not just a question of having a woman outside that you love; otherwise things would have been less complicated.

In India we have the concept of ARDHANARISHWAR. That corresponds to the Taoist approach of Yin and Yang.

Shiva has been sculpted, painted as both half – man, half – woman. Half of his body is that of a man and half of his body is that of a woman. When for the first time those statues were discovered by the West, the West laughed – it looked so absurd. What is the point of it? Now they have understood what the point of it is. It is one of the most fundamental things of life.

So are you, just like Shiva, half-half.

Unless one transcends this inner polarity one will not attain to the One, one will remain two.

In ordinary life, we remain dual. And in the space of twenty-four hours we change many times from one pole to the other. Watch. We may be a man, but sometimes we are very feminine, very vulnerable. We may be a woman, but sometimes in the daytime we are very masculine. When the woman is masculine, she becomes very very aggressive – more aggressive than any man can ever be, because her aggressiveness is very fresh, unused, and just like unused land is very fertile. And so is the case with man. If a man is tender, he is very tender – more than the woman, because that is unused soil, that part of his being has not been used; it is fresh, very alive. So this strange phenomenon is observed again and again if one becomes a little watchful.

Woman generally loves; man does not generally love. Woman is only sometimes quarrelsome, but when she is, then she really is. Man only sometimes loves, but when he does he really does. Those are the unused parts of their being. When they are used, they have freshness.

This inner polarity keeps one in a kind of anguish, conflict; without it one cannot exist. The One remains invisible – that's why God is invisible. To become visible the One has to become two.

God is invisible. If he wants to become man and woman, he will have to become two, he will have to become matter and spirit, he will have to become body and soul, he will have to become this and that. Only the two are visible. The world consists of the 'two.' The world is dual. And the moment one can manage to make this duality disappear in oneness, one will become invisible. It has great significance, but it is a metaphor.

Neem Karoli Baba was both visible and invisible. His form was visible, the formless was invisible. Only the dual can be seen, the non-dual becomes unseen.

God has to become two, only then the game, the play is possible. Ancient Indian scriptures say he felt very lonely. He longed for the other, that's why he became two. He became man and woman, cow and bull, and so on and so forth. The whole existence is sexual. By 'sexual' is meant dual. The whole existence is sexual. That is why the sun is represented as being male and the moon as being female. It is not poetry; it is fact.

In Christian theology, things are not so deep, they are very superficial. In Christian theology, we have only creation. What about de-creation? How can there be creation without de-creation? In the Eastern theology, they are both together: SRISHTI means creation; PRALAYA means de-creation. Vishnu and Shiva are symbols of life and death.

There is a moment when God becomes manifest, and then there is a moment when God becomes unmanifested again – all disappears into nothingness.

The male and the feminine principle are very fundamental to Hinduism. That is why with every God there is a consort, a female Shakti.

Meditation and Prayer are two ways to grow consciousness. Meditation is walking alone; prayer needs a divine support for surrender. Meditation and prayer takes one to Love.

Neem Karoli Baba was love personified.

External Stimuli and Internal Reactions

In the foregoing pages, I have tried to describe the human mind, misery and anxiety from the western psychology perspective and also through the yoga system of Patanjali.

Both the methods have been tried out to help man come out of misery and anxiety.

But Yoga method is ancient; it was based on raising human energy level through spiritual practices leading to Samadhi. It has been lost in oblivion and is difficult to practise in modern times i.e. "Kaliyuga."

Psychotherapy is a modern western method to deal with mental issues.

But the psychotherapy is based on the law of cause and effect.

The therapist tries to establish the cause and then treats the client according to his skill.

The law of cause and effect works in the realm of matter. If you heat water to 100 degree centigrade, it will vaporize. That is the law which is applicable anywhere.

But mind is not matter. Western psychologists tried to determine the cause by developing a model of the mind. Their method was that certain desires are hidden deep in the mind as repression. If these repressions are thrown out of the system, one can live blissfully. Sigmund Freud developed his theories analyzing dreams and relating them to suppressed sex. Many others experimented with different theories. Psychedelic drugs were tried to bring a person to an altered state of consciousness. Neuropsychiatrists use anti-depressant drugs to bring the client to sleep and drowsiness.

Human mind is affected by the external stimuli. The cause of the stimuli is outside and the effect of reaction is inside.

If somebody abuses me, I react either with more intensity or suppress my anger if I find the other stronger. These reactions are instinctive. These are uncontrolled. It cannot be willed. Sex is also such an instinct. It cannot be willed.

Hindus long time ago knew that man was under the control of nature's forces. The seers knew that so long as man was a victim of nature, he would suffer. Various spiritual practices were developed to transcend nature's forces of sex, anger, greed etc.

On the contrary, western analytical methods work on the theory of cause and effect. It fits well in the investigation of matter. Descartes was the founder of this theory followed by Newton and others who devoted their life in the service of science and mathematics. They propounded some hypothesis and went on to prove the correctness of the hypothesis.

For example, Euclid postulated some hypothesis in geometry. He defined point as that which has **"no width, no length and no depth."**

From this definition the entire edifice of geometry was developed. Euclid's axioms are no longer true.

The whole of science depends on the theory of cause and effect. You create the cause and the effect follows. Life is a causal link. You put the seed in the soil and it will sprout. If the cause is there, then the tree will follow. The fire is there – you put your hand in it and it will burn. The cause is there and the effect will follow. You take poison and you will die. You arrange for the cause and the effect follows.

This is one of the most basic scientific laws that cause and effect is the innermost link of all processes of life. Religion knows about a second law, which is still deeper than this. But the second law which is deeper than this will look absurd.

Religion says: Produce the effect and the cause follows. This is absolutely absurd in scientific terms.

Science says: If the cause is there, the effect follows. Religion says the converse is also true: you create the effect, and see…the cause follows.

There is a situation in which you feel happy. A friend has come, a beloved has called. A situation is the cause – you feel happy. Happiness is the effect. The coming of the beloved is the cause.

Religion says: Be happy and the beloved comes. Create the effect and the cause follows. The second law is more basic than the first. Just be happy and the beloved comes. Just be happy, and friends are there.

Just be happy and everything follows.

Jesus says the same thing in different words: "Seek ye first the Kingdom of God, then all else will follow.

But the Kingdom of God is the end, the effect. Seek ye first the end – end means the effect, the result – and the cause will follow. This is as it should be.

It is not only that you place a seed in the soil and the tree follows; let there be a tree and there are millions of seeds. If cause is followed by effect, effect is again followed by cause. This is the chain!

Then it becomes a circle – start from anywhere, create the cause or create the effect.

It is easier to create the effect because the effect depends totally upon you; the cause may not be so dependent on you. If you say you can only be happy when a certain friend is there, then it depends on a certain friend, whether he is there or not. If I say I cannot be happy until I attain this much wealth, then it depends on the whole world and the economic situations and everything.

It may not happen, and then I cannot be happy.

Cause is beyond me. Effect is within me. Cause is in the surroundings, in the situations – cause is without. EFFECT IS ME! If I can create the effect, the cause will follow.

Choose happiness – that means you are choosing the effect – and then see what happens. Choose ecstasy and see what happens. Choose to be blissful and see what happens. Your whole life will change immediately and you will see **miracles** happening around you – because now you have created the effect and causes will have to follow.

This will look magical; you can even call it the law of magic. The first is the law of science and the second is the law of magic. Religion is magic, and you can be the magician.

Create the effect and see what happens; causes immediately surround you, they follow. Don't wait for the causes; you have waited long enough. Choose happiness and you will be happy.

What is the problem? Why can't you choose? Why can't you work on this law? Because your mind, the whole mind, which has been trained by scientific thinking, says that if you are not happy and you try to be happy, that happiness will be artificial. If you are not happy and you try to be happy that will be just acting, that will not be real. This is what scientific thinking says that that will not be real, you will be just acting.

If you try, then try wholeheartedly. Don't remain behind, move into it, become the acting – dissolve the actor into acting and then see what happens. It will become the real and then you will feel it is spontaneous. You have not done it; you will know then that it has happened. But unless you are total this cannot happen. Create the effect, be in it completely, and then see and observe the results.

Like psychotherapy, **communism** was another effort to solve the anxiety and worry arising out of the inequality of wealth distribution.

Communism postulated that the cause was money. And if money is taken away from the individual and given to the state the misery would be over. There is no need for a God or a divinity.

But communism failed because it was trying to remove the cause and bring in the effect. When money power goes in the hands of the state, it is dictatorship of the proletariat. The world has seen the collapse of communism and the way it became dictatorial in the hands of a few who controlled money, science and technology.

Similar things are happening in **Socialist** economies. The government still controls large part of money under the control of capitalists.

And as far as **capitalist** economies are concerned, they control the elected representatives, media, resources, wealth of nations without any external war, which famous Scottish economist Adam Smith called "invisible hands." It is not the "well being" of the people; it is profit motive that breeds greed.

All these efforts to rid man out of worry have failed because these were not based upon any positive energy. What the world needs today is to work more on the effect than on the cause.

Cause is beyond us. Effect is within us.

There is an old saying: Weep and you weep alone, laugh and the world laughs with you. Even the trees, the rocks, the sand, the clouds, if you can create the effect and be ecstatic, they will all dance with you; then the whole existence becomes a dance, a celebration.

But it depends on you, if you can create the effect. It is the easiest thing possible. It looks very difficult because we have not tried it yet.

Prayer

How can one pray to God? You don't know God – that's why you are praying. You would like to know what God is, but you don't know. That's why you are pouring your heart out. It is waiting for the unknown to take possession of you. This is faith, this is trust.

The sceptical mind wants first to be certain whether there is a God.

"We will pray only if God exists" – then you will never pray, because you will never know without praying that God exists. You have made an impossible condition for praying. It is not to be fulfilled. You have to pray. Don't ask the question whether God exists or not. God is irrelevant at this point. At this point, make prayer possible.

That is what Neem Karoli Baba said, "Recite Sita – Ram, Sita – Ram," Sundarkand and Hanuman Chalisa, even if you have to recite mechanically, even if you don't have trust. Trust would come by and by with the purity of heart."

Prayer is a song of the heart addressed to the unknown. Maybe he is, maybe he is not, but that is not the point. One is joyous in pouring one's heart out. It is a joy unto itself. Whether God exists or not is secondary. Prayer is primary. And when prayer is primary, it reveals God, it opens your eyes. It creates God. Suddenly the world becomes afire when you are afire. When your heart is aflame, suddenly you see the whole world aflame with the divine, with the unknown, with the mysterious.

I was on the path of meditation. I questioned about the existence of God? Unless I know God, how can I pray?

And then suddenly Neem Karoli Baba came into my life. The more I read about him the more convinced I became about the existence of God. I became a theist.

Neem Karoli Baba has sown the seeds of God.

That is why I want the entire world to know about him.

There are innumerable causes that are creating misery on this planet. We can keep on analyzing the causes but would never be able to remove it.

Spirituality is Creating the Effect Instead of Working on the Causes

Throughout my life, I was trying to analyze the causes and finding remedies. But I failed.

I therefore strongly advocate spirituality instead of psychotherapeutic methods or other methods that are working directly on the causes. Hinduism has worked on the balancing of inner energy that is not detectable by the modern medical science. For Hinduism, body and mind is an organic and whole, but for modern medical science, finding the cause in the parts is primary aim. It works well with the body but not with the mind.

Control of money through complex network of banking system, fractional reserve banking, interest on lending, debt-based economy, increased taxation, control of science and technology, media, climate control, excavation of nature's resources from the earth, nuclear weapons and hosts of other things are creating havoc on this planet. It is impossible to eliminate these causes by human efforts. Only if God incarnates on this planet, these demonic forces could be eliminated to establish order. But man can still be saved individually through spiritual support, prayer and devotion to Lord Hanuman, who is "Sankat Mochan."

Rama and Hanuman as a Universal God and Deity

Hindu incarnations of God and deity need to be understood by rest of the world. As already established, Rama is an incarnation of God who solves global issues by killing demonic forces. Hanuman is a deity, an incarnation, a devotee of Rama to take care of the individuals who are living in hopeless situations. Neem Karoli Baba is an incarnation of Hanuman. Through his human form, Baba was able to establish trust in Rama and Hanuman

Establishment of Ashrams and Temples Throughout the World

As I have already pointed out, the west under the influence of science and technology has lost moorings in trust in God. The Abrahamic God died when **Nietzsche** proclaimed "God is dead." This was followed by existentialist philosophers.

Today the west needs a God. Let the west learn from India.

Neem Karoli Baba has shown the model of Ashrams and temples. Let these be established throughout the world. These Ashrams and temples should be established in forests or mountainous regions, high energy places, where one can experience divine energy, silence and prayer. Ashrams can be a place where one can spend a short time, say three days and return to the world fully rejuvenated. An Ashram should be managed by trusts through voluntary donations. Any devotee should be able to stay free of cost for a short period of, say, three days and given vegetarian neat and clean food. Prayer, devotional music and chanting should create high – energy field. No difficult yogic spiritual practices are needed.

The entire activity should be based on service. Service should come out of one's heart. It should not become a ritual. Service is not a motive like a profit motive. Service is a reward all by itself.

Statues of Lord Rama, Hanuman, Vishnu, Lakshmi, Shiva and Parvati, and Neem Karoli Baba made of marble should be established in temples for "Arati" and prayer for the residents. Intoxicants, non-vegetarian foods should not be allowed. People should maintain strict silence. No mobile phones or cameras should be allowed. Anybody coming as a tourist should be told in strict terms to follow the rules.

This would be a great service to mankind and would uplift the energy of this planet.

In the end, I wish the readers of this book to be showered with the grace of Lord so that they can come out of hopelessness and lead a blissful life. That, in my opinion, is the aim of all spirituality.

Epilogue

Religion and spirituality are polar opposites.

Religion is based on belief system.

Spirituality is based upon trust. It comes with individual effort. No effort is needed to be religious. It comes to humans through birth and special structure.

India is not dogamatic. It has experimented in spirituality. It has been a land of masters and discsiples and Gods and devotees. Gods incarnate on this planet in human form to bring trust in spirituality.

Without a spiritual support humans would suffer.

Neem Karoli Baba is an incarnation of Lord Hanuman. Hanuman is a devotee of Rama.

The concept of master/disciple and incarnations is nowhere in the world except in India.

This book is intended to introduce to a western reader about Hindu concept of spirituality.

Western readers free of prejudices and preconceived notions can grasp Indian spirituality more than the Indian readers who carry the burden of knowledge since the ancient past.

Western mind is analytical. But, it has lost touch with heart and feelings.

This must be revived, if the man is to be made healthy. Man has become sick. Western techniques of psychotherapy and alternative therapies are proving unsuccessful because they are not based on devotion but are analytical based on resoning.

Devotion is an Energy phenomenon. If one is around an enlightened master, and receptive, one can feel the high state of energy.

I hope this book would help the western seeker to understand spirituality and the high energy phenomenon.

Siice ancient times, saints in India moved to the Himalayas and lived in caves. These cavees though appear unhyugenic were highenergy fields.

In the recent times, one famous wetern psycghologist Dr. Wilhelm Reich (1897–1957) did an experiment in high energy field. He called this energy "Orgone Energy." It is the same energy which is called "Prana Energy" in Yoga. Dr. Reich constructed a chamber where a patient with mental problems could sit for a few hours and experience high energy field. Deficit of Orgone energy was the root cause of several diseases.

In India temples, prayer and chanting are for the purpose of raising elan vital or "Prana Energy."

The story of Rama, Sita, Ravana, Lakshman and Hanuman can be symbolized with modern psychology. Rama is our soul; Sita is the heart, full of love. Ravana symbolizes intellect. The intellect overpowers heart and dominates. Hanuman is the intuition which salvages heart from the intellect. Intution i.e. Hanuman is in the sevice of Soul which is Rama. Lakshman represents our consciousness.

Neem Karoli Baba is an incarnation of Hanuman. He revived trust in Hanuman through his grace and helped millions to overcome mundane issues.